Writings by Tom Johnson

You Are Always Your Own Experience
Your Creative Self
To Love or To Be Loved
The Power of Surrender
How Not To Be Lonely
Your Right To Be Illogical
What Religious Science Is

LOS ARBOLES PUBLICATIONS
P.O. Box 7000-54
Redondo Beach, California
90277
FIRST EDITION

Dedication

I gratefully dedicate this book to Dr. Raymond Charles Barker, who opened wide the door to the great Power of Mind for me. His influence started me gloriously on my endless journey of Self-discovery.

THE
SHADOWS
OF YOUR
MIND

Tom Johnson

COVER ILLUSTRATION
AND
BOOK DESIGN
by
Norman Merritt

Library of Congress Cataloging in Publication Data
Johnson, Tom, date–
The shadows of your mind.

1. New Thought. I. Title.
BF639.J575 1983   230'.998   83-762
ISBN 0-941992-02-0

Contents

Introduction

The world is always to us what we are to ourselves. All that we see and hear is merely our own interpretation. Everything that happens can be to us whatever we choose. It is up to each of us to accept the responsibility for our happiness.

Within our own consciousness are shadows that get in the way of our seeing clearly and distinctly the great beauty and wonder of the world, of each and every experience. But there is an exciting way to brush away those shadows and to experience everything in such a way that life is a magnificent adventure, free of the shadows.

I have written this book with beginner and advance student in mind. For those who are not familiar with my terminology, let me make a few clarifications:

I separate and capitalize Self because the Self is what we are. It is consciousness, It is our identity, It is the power in our life.

Mind is capitalized because It is the creative power. Mind not only creates, but It has within Itself all intelligence, all ideas that are ours to use. Mind is directed always by the Self.

Principle is the Law of Mind directed at the level of our God-Self and every time we use an idea of limitation, we are out of Principle.

Truth is made up of those ideas that enhance and fulfill our lives. All ideas that we use become form, but Truth always sets us free. Truth directs Mind by means of Its creative good. Truth permits us to live fully, while an idea of limitation always causes Mind to create an experience of that limitation.

Treatment or Scientific Prayer is the conscious and deliberate use of Truth. When we know that Mind is meant to be directed and always creates what we choose, then we can definitely and deliberately use Mind for our creative purposes.

As you continue to read and assimilate the true meaning behind the written word, trust that the shadows will disappear.

Tom Johnson

Acknowledgments

I am eternally grateful to Susan George for her invaluable help and suggestions with the refinement of this book. She gave of her great expertise and time with much love and enthusiasm.

I count as one of my many blessings, the faith demonstrated by Jean Beckman, President of Los Arboles Publications, in my presentation of the Science of Mind. Her dedication to the teaching of Truth and the great power within us all, has made it possible for me to reach a wide new audience.

CHAPTER I

The Shadows of Your Mind

If we are honest with ourselves, we will all have to admit that we have found ourselves reacting to what others have said or done at one time or another. In reacting we have unwittingly and unconsciously indicated that someone else is a power or the power in our life. We have, in some way, said that someone is cause to our experience. But in our experience who should come first? We or someone else? In acknowledging the mental law of cause and effect we must admit that there is always a cause to our every experience. Since we stand at the center of our every experience we have got to admit that the cause is always our own Self. No one else can be cause to our experience even though we may believe that he or she is. You and I think, feel and express, and Mind causes our experience to take place, created out of what we ourselves choose to think, feel and reveal. The people in our world are there as reflections of our own Self. They are shadows in our own use of Mind.

When we react to the actions of others we are saying, in essence, that our good comes from outside of our Self, or that we have to overcome or do something about the power "out there." The truth is that we can never do anything about anyone or about any thing, for in our experience they are but shadows of our use of Mind. When we react we are saying that there is our own Self AND something or someone else. However, in our expression of life there is only SELF. We only see that which is within our own consciousness. The people and things in our life are but shadows of the Mind. They are only as real as we permit them to be as being cause to our experience.

When we try to help someone, to heal someone, we are using an idea of limitation about that someone. The idea, however, is within our own consciousness. We may believe that this is true about them, this disease, poverty, or fear, but we then fail to realize that the power in our experience is our own Self, our own beliefs. We then try to change, to overcome, or to get someone to agree with us. The effects in our life are still effects, whether they be people or things. The law of our Self is still drawing into our life those people who help us experience our own Self, our beliefs. We are still seeing, within them, that which is within our own Self first of all.

Should we need to have others agree with us all the time, or even part of the time, that need is still within our own Self. That need then creates an experience of that need. No one can ever really agree with us because each person has his own thoughts, his own purpose, his own level of consciousness. "But," you say, "I thought you just said that they are in my life to help me experience my Self. Why then are they so disagreeable?" Are they really disagreeable? That is merely what we may see. That is our own interpretation. If we are insecure in our own Selfhood, then there is going to be a need for agreement. The need, the desire, the demand for it, will never permit agreement, and the person is still but a shadow in your use of Mind.

In trying to get someone to agree with us, we are

13

reacting to a shadow. Our belief that this other person is cause to our experience is but a shadow. We are reacting to a belief. Our belief is something within our own consciousness. Since we only see and hear through our own beliefs, then consciousness must become form, since that is the way Mind works, to reflect those beliefs. We always interpret what we see and hear through our own identity, our own beliefs. Someone else may see the same thing and interpret it altogether differently. We each have our own interpretation and they are different. Who is right? We are both right for ourselves.

We are not here to fight, argue, overcome or to change the world. We are here to realize that there is a law in action and it is always a law of our own Self.

As we consciously acknowledge the greatness, the uniqueness, of our Self, and act accordingly, the world must respond to us in kind for it is the law that what we give out first of all must come back to us. Factually, it is doing so already; it always has and always will. The people in our world helping us out in fulfilling our dreams, our desires, our fears, or whatever. They are merely reacting to whatever we are doing, thinking, feeling and expressing. Whatever we are reacting against has no real power. The power is always within our own Self. The power in our life is always our Self, whatever that Self may be seen to be.

What we are reacting to has absolutely no power. It is a shadow. What we think people are doing they are not really doing. What we see is not necessarily true for we always see through a state of mind, through our anxiety, fear, love, joy or whatever is the level of our consciousness. We are forever imposing our Self upon everything in our life, every person in our life. We are always interpreting everything that happens through our own consciousness. If we have ever been upset when someone did not agree with us, we have proved this point. If someone did agree with us and we were filled with a sense of elation and joy, we have proved it again. Our need to have them agree with us is what caused us to be unhappy or happy. Our need to have something happen the way we want it to happen reveals our insecurity about our own Self. When we demand that the world conform to what we want simply means that we are referring to our Self in a limited way.

One time I said, "I love you," to someone and she reacted with great anger. She had not really heard what I said. She heard something altogether different. What she heard was within her Self. Every one of us has been misquoted. What we did say may have been quoted verbatim but there was an added tone of derision supplied by the person impersonating us, and therefore it was not what we really said at all. We ourselves often mishear what others are saying. We are hearing our own consciousness.

People are always saying to us, "I love you." In reality, they are saying, "Please love me." They are saying this in one way or another regardless of what the outer projection may seem to be. If we hear something else, then we are hearing something from within our own consciousness. We are imposing upon our Self an interpretation. We are projecting our Self upon them and this projection is a shadow of our own consciousness. Does it not seem ridiculous to react to a shadow, to an illusion, to something within our own Self that we believe to be "out there?"

In our Self-awareness, there cannot be Self AND something else. There can only be Self AS. There cannot be our consciousness AND our work, home, mate, money, etc. There is only our consciousness AS. In my experience, there is not me and you. There is only me. If you are in my life, then you are in my life as my interpretation of you. You are there because of the law of my own Self, and I am always really seeing that which is within my own consciousness. The things in our life represent our taste, our desires, our level of self-accceptance, or they would not be there. We are seeing, hearing, and experiencing our own consciousness, which becomes form. The "things" that are "out there" are really "within."

Many people look at the same object or the same person and they all see something different. They see it as good, bad, so-so, nice, lovely, ugly, or whatever. But to each one it is at least slightly different. That object or that person is to each one what they are to themselves. We are always seeing our own Self. If we are critical of others, it is because we are critical of ourselves. If we are understanding of others, it is because we do not sit in judgment upon our own Self. We go to a movie and it is a different experience for each of us. Some people laugh and some cry at the same scene. Some do not react at all. We are experiencing the uniqueness that we are, but what we are laughing or crying at is but a shadow. A shadow of the Mind. It has no absolute reality. We, ourselves, give it a seeming reality because of our belief. Because of what we believe we are seeing. It is still a shadow.

When we are fighting or arguing with someone, when we are loving someone, when we believe that we are dealing with people, we are really working with our Self, with the shadows of our Mind. There is only Self in our experience. We may have accepted beliefs from others, but we ourselves are now using them, so they are now ours. When we let go and no longer try to fight someone, as we no longer try to get someone to agree with us, and, instead, put our attention on Who and What we really ARE, then we are free to see through the consciousness of love, of our True Self, of the greatness and uniqueness that we really are.

Marriage is not meant to be an excuse to express violence, anger or resentment. All of these come from within the individual. When we attach ourselves to someone, seeking security and love from them, we are creating our own problems. We are sowing the seeds of anger and resentment within our own Self. When we attach ourselves to someone in terms of wanting them to agree with us, in having to be with them all of the time, something begins to happen and we begin to hate that to which we are attached. When we love someone, there is no attachment. There is release. When we do not demand that others agree with our own interpretations, there is no possibility of violence. When we love we appreciate the other's viewpoint and demand that their needs be met as well as ours.

When we are insecure about our Self, we have thought about our Self in a limited way. We then feel we have to reach out and clutch, grasp, try to own, possess, dominate and try to get others to agree with us. This has nothing whatever to do with love. Love is freedom. Love releases the people in our world to be the only thing they can be, themselves. Love causes us to be about the business of living out of our own integrity, our own sense of completeness, out of the inner resources that we ourselves have to give. Mind then takes over and creates the forms, the things, the people, the opportunities that reflect that love.

In seeking anything from someone we are saying in effect that they are cause rather than the effect in our life. In looking for our good from someone, we are dealing with the shadow rather than the reality. Our good comes from within our Self, never from someone else. It may seem to come from someone but, in reality, it comes because of what is first of all within our consciousness. It may come through them, but it always comes from our own Self.

The love that we give to someone else is really directed to our own Self. The violence that we try to inflict upon someone else is also really directed to our own Self. All of this takes place because of self-love or self-hate; self-acceptance or self-rejection; a sense of completeness or a sense of inadequacy. Even when we think that we are focusing our attention upon someone else, we are thinking through our own self-image. That thought, that feeling, goes into subconscious Mind and Mind is sending back to us that which reflects our own thought. There is no such thing as someone else arguing with us. We are always arguing with our Self.

When we fail to acknowledge the fullness and greatness of our Self, we are using a self-image that is made up of the mistakes of yesterday. Our feelings of inadequacy then demand that someone else agree with us when they cannot. Even if they try to, we cannot see it in that way. We are again dealing with a shadow in our own consciousness.

As we let go of the people in our world as being cause to our experience and realize that it is all created out of our own Self, then we are releasing the shadows of the Mind. We are no longer depending on that shadow when we do this. There are all kinds of people, but each one is still an individualization of life, of God. We ourselves determine their value in our own experience. This is something that we ourselves impose upon them.

When we depend upon someone, we are leaning upon our desires, needs, and interpretation. We can never really depend upon someone for the reason that dependency causes Mind to create the experience of disagreement or imitation.

The person we depend upon is always going to disappoint us in some way. What is really happening when we do this is that we are demanding something of them.

We are seeking to get, and thus Mind creates the experience of taking away since we only have what we give. Our seeking anything from anyone causes Mind to create an experience of disagreement within our own Self.

There is no power out there in the world of effect. It is always within. Mind is ALWAYS creating the experience of our own consciousness. Our Self is all that we really have. Everything in our experience is created out of it. When we are giving, sharing, revealing our SELF-ACCEPTANCE, our SELF-SUFFICIENCY, our SELF-RELIANCE, asking nothing of anyone, then the law of Mind is going to bring into our life the right opportunities and those people who correspond and reflect our Self.

No longer make demands upon anyone and we release them as being cause to our experience. Thus we are no longer fighting or trying to overcome those shadows of the mind that we once believed to be power. Be self-aware and we are then consciously at one with that Self that is already and forever complete. Be in tune with that Self that has never made a mistake and never will make a mistake. Be self-aware and actively know that we are individualizations of nothing less than God.

We do not have to go after anything or anyone. We can let the law of attraction take care of that for us. This does not mean that we do not take action, for it is the action of our Self that draws to us the forms of that action. But we can use our thought to acknowledge the WHOLENESS of our Self, and thus we do not need to lean upon or try to attach ourselves to anyone or any thing. In BEING our Self, our relationships with others can be open and free and creative. These relationships can be ones of love rather than of possession, domination, manipulation or attachment. Since no one can ever really agree with you, let go of that approach. Relationships are not meant to be made out of agreement, but of revealing the authenticity of each person. It is meant to be an experience of sharing, of giving, of permitting each to explore and grow and unfold. The other person's needs do not have to be our needs, yet we must help him or her fulfill those needs. Each person must be fulfilled in any relationship.

In any and every relationship we need to remember that we only have our own Self to give and to share. And what we give is what we have. Self-discovery is meant to free us in the full expression of our own uniqueness. Love does not demand agreement. It does not demand that everyone else must whip into shape and do exactly what we want them to do. It does not mean that we live happily ever after in a blissful experience of total togetherness. It means that there is individuality experienced for each person. It means growth, challenges, respect, sharing, understanding.

We can only demonstrate the job, the work, the things, of our own Self. We can only have in our life the people who represent our Self, what we are individually giving and exuding. Consciousness always becomes form. If we love and respect our own Self, and are using our thought correctly about WHO and WHAT we REALLY are, then Mind must create the forms and the experience of that Self. If we are giving the highest and truest of our Self to all that we are doing, then we must have in our experience the job, the work, the people, things and body that corresponds to what we are giving. This is the way that Mind works.

We are told in the Bible to resist not evil. Why? Evil is nothing but a shadow. It is no thing. If we believe in evil, we are the victim of that belief. There is still no power outside of our own Self. We are always bound by our own interpretation, which is always within our own Self. We always interpret everything and everyone in the only way that we can. Through the eyes of our own Self. What we resist or try to overcome is controlling us. It is but a shadow.

Usually when we protest loudly about the way others are behaving it means that we would really like to be doing the same thing, only our patterns of guilt have been established to keep us from doing it. Those who appoint themselves as the authority about others' behavior are trying to build their own self-esteem. Their need to be judgmental is a shadow getting in the way of the growth of the Self.

No one is ever withholding our good. This is an impossibility. That which represents our consciousness must be in our life in one way or another. No one has the power to give or to take away. Our own consciousness cannot be denied. Mind is ALWAYS creating the forms and experience of our own Self. This is why we can never really do anything about someone else. This is why we must always work on our own Self, on our identity, our own behavior, our own consciousness.

You may say, "I would love to have this particular house, or that salary, or that person in my life. If Mind creates, then why do I not have them?" Since we always have that which represents our own consciousness, the good that we desire we do not have because we have not as yet earned it by right of consciousness. We have to be equal to it before we can have it. If we already have the consciousness for it, and are revealing that consciousness always, then we must already have the people and things that represent it. If our good seems to elude us, it is because we are looking outside of our own Self for this good, when all the while all that we can ever use and desire is already within our Self. We must simply awaken to it and live it.

Mind is forever creating opportunity after opportunity which will permit us to give of our Self, whatever we see that Self to be. If we do not accept those opportunities and give, then we do not receive. If we do not believe in our Self, and if we are not giving and sharing of this fullness and greatness that we really are, then how can we possibly expect to receive what we really want in return? The moment that we acknowledge our unique individuality of completeness and move into action in the expression of it, in that very moment Mind must provide the forms that reflect this now activity of Being. It creates the body that is the ideal vehicle of this Self and its expression. Our own expression.

Right where we are, right now, ALL OF LIFE IS. Right where we are, right now, True Self is. If we do not acknowledge and express it, we are then acknowledging and expressing another concept. But whatever we are expressing, Mind is even now creating the outward reflection. Everything in our life right now is but a shadow of our own use of thought, feeling and expression.

Most of us have felt or believe that someone else was keeping our good from coming into our life. We have blamed others for the things that have happened to us. We have blamed them if we lost our job, if someone left us, if we got sick, if we were late, etc. We have often gotten upset or angry with them. But there is no one who can withhold our good. Our consciousness is always attracting to us all that reflects our now level of consciousness and its expression. Absolutely no one can get in the way of this taking place. If we believe that they can, then this belief is a shadow and we experience that shadow. The belief that someone can give to us something or take it away is an illusion, a shadow of the Mind. We can only experience our own interpretation, and as we let go of looking to anything or for anything from anyone, we will be free to be Self aware, we will be able to give creatively to the present moment.

When we live and express out of true Self-awareness, we are functioning in a world where there is no competition and no comparison. Others may be experiencing it, but not anyone who is the action of being his or her own Self of uniqueness. The belief in competition is an idea of limitation. It is a shadow of the Mind. There is no competition for we can only experience our own Self, our own consciousness. This may sound like a very repetitive idea, but it is one that has to be emphasized until we really accept it and understand it. No one can take away our business, no one can take away that which belongs to us by right of consciousness. No one can take away our mate, job, money. If they seem to, it wasn't ours to keep. In order to attain and maintain in our life our good, we must ever be living and expressing the Truth that permits that good to stay. Others may believe that they are competing with you, but that is their belief and therefore that is their own experience. Each person is drawing to himself, because of the way that Mind works, that which fits and corresponds to his or her level of consciousness right now.

We might say, "But I've gone after a particular job and discovered that there were all kinds of people after the same job. They were all doing all kinds of things to make sure that they got that job. Isn't that competition?" No. Each person demonstrates his own work, his own good. If that job belongs to you by right of consciousness, nothing on this earth can keep it from you. If others are trying to force something to happen, then force must be maintained to keep their good. However, just because we do not believe in competition does not mean that we just sit around and wait for something to happen. In order to put the law of Being into action, we must express. Being means action.

We must know Who and What we really are and then fill each moment with the power of this Self. The What are those qualities of the ideal that each one of us has. Each moment is filled with our level of self-esteem, with our self-image, and the motivation of it. What we cast upon the waters always comes back to us. It is our purpose to always be building the consciousness of success, love, Truth and to then let that consciousness guide and direct our way into greater giving, into more honest, authentic and loving creative expression. Consciousness must always become form.

There is always the right and ideal job for each of us. Mind is always creating exactly what we are. As long as we have the highest possible concept of our Self, Mind must create the equivalent at the level of effect in our life. If we do not already have what we consider to be the ideal job, then we cannot blame the world. The world has nothing to do with anything. The world is always responding to what we are giving. To blame the world is to blame a shadow, for the world is merely an experience of our own interpretation. When we are reacting to the world and what it seems to be doing, we are reacting to our own belief, to our interpretation. Yet all the while, Mind is creating a NOW opportunity for us to express either the GENIUS that each of us really is, or whatever self-image we do have.

Many of us believe that we are limited in our work, our jobs, our marital relationships, or any area of success, by the level of our education. We believe that we are limited to the experience we have already had and therefore when we look for a new job we believe that we must stay in the same field. Many believe that they are limited by their present state of health. We may believe that we are being held back because we have no particular talent. If we believe any of these, we are letting our experience be created out of these beliefs and we are stuck in the status quo. But—there is not a word of truth in any of those beliefs. Why let your life be controlled by a shadow? Why take yourself out of the mainstream of life because of a shadow, because of an illusion?

There is something within us that really KNOWS what to do, what to say, what to give, what to express. There is that within each of us that is absolutely magnificent, that which is magnificently unique and very special. The world wants it and needs it. However, if we are not actively aware of it, if we do not acknowledge it, then it cannot be alive either in our consciousness or in our experience. Our beliefs, our acknowledgement, our self-acceptance level is what we live by. Mind is always creating the forms of it. If we are using beliefs of limitation, these are but shadows of the mind that are controlling us simply because we accept them.

Can a shadow cause us to act or react in a particular way? Of course it can if we believe it to be so. When we are thinking, living, and acting out of our True Self, there is absolutely no competition for that which we live causes Mind to create the opportunities, the job, of that uniqueness which we are. Mind manifests our beliefs in every area of our life. Mind creates the things and the people of our Self always. Say to yourself:

"I dare to be my Self. In knowing that there is but One Self, and that I am an individualization of It, this Self that God is as me, there is always that within me that has something positive and creative to give to each and every moment. I cease looking to the world for my good and realize that all good is already within my Self. There is neither competition nor comparison in my use of thought for I am not a repetition of anyone in any way. I am unique, I am special, I am life forever unfolding as me."

If we have ever compared ourselves to anyone, we have always come out second best, even if we think that we are better than others. The need to compare says that we are insecure about our Self in some way and this feeling causes Mind to create accordingly. If we know Who and What we truly are, and are aware of the true COM-PLETENESS and PERFECTION of our Self, there would then never be any need to compare. Not only would there not be the need, but there would not be the action. Our comparison says that we believe that there is our own Self AND someone else. But there is only ONE. The people in our life all represent some aspect of our own Self. In our own experience there is only Self, and all of the people and things in our life are our consciousness become form.

When we use treatment, meditation, or prayer to oppose, deny or to fight anyone or anything, we are using it to fight a shadow, because nothing is ever opposing us. The law of our Being is always creating for us. The world is always in agreement, even though it may seem to us to be the contrary. If we are looking for a fight, we will always find it. Mind will demonstrate or provide the right person in the right way to argue with us, to fight with us. Actually, it is something that we are doing to our own Self. The world is reacting to us and is giving us exactly what we are asking for because of our attitude or belief. Even if someone else speaks the first word and insults us, or even though someone else strikes the first blow, it is our own consciousness that has drawn that person into our life. They are shadows. The reality or the cause is within our own Self. There is absolutely nothing in our life, in our experience but Self.

When we try to impose our beliefs upon others, we are acting out of inner insecurity. When we see insufficiency, insecurity, incompleteness within others, what are we really seeing through? We are looking through our own needs, through our own consciousness. Parents very often have children to fulfill their own needs rather than helping those children to fulfill theirs. When we see imperfection within someone else we are seeing a shadow. It is a shadow of our own fear, doubt or insecurity. We are imposing it upon that someone. Others may not see it at all because they do not have a need to see it. The truth is that every person, no matter who they are, is an individualization of life, of God. In our own experience, those people are to us what we are to ourselves.

If we see all kinds of negative, stupid and unreliable people in our life, why do we have that need to see these qualities in so many people? They are going to react to us or be to us exactly what we see them to be. By our judgments we are imposing something within our Self upon others and it is not fair to them unless we are seeing through the consciousness of love, for love makes no judgments. Mind is always creating the experience of our own Self, which is what we are seeing, hearing and believing about our Self. What you believe about someone else is what you must have within your own experience in one way or another because our beliefs are an activity within our own consciousness. When we struggle to hold on to someone or to some thing, we are really setting up ourselves to be rejected. This shadow is a belief that our good is outside of our Self. Struggle is a result of a belief that we are not already complete. It is an action of a low level of Self-esteem.

Whenever we do not like ourselves or feel very insecure about our Self, we seek to add to ourselves by bringing into our lives more and better people, and an endless array of things. But things and people do not bring us happiness. Happiness comes from our facing challenges and going through them with our own inner reserves, by thinking for ourselves and by giving rather than trying to get.

What we go after we never really have. We only really have what we express, what we give. The struggle to overcome or even to maintain says, in effect, "I am not complete. I do not know who Who and What I am."

Insecurity, a sense of incompleteness, is always a result of looking at our Self incorrectly. This insecurity always attaches itself to person, place or thing, and is therefore never secure because things and people do not create security. They are there to correspond, to respond, to our level of self-esteem. When we believe in our Self, in the great sufficiency of this Self, we let go of the "effects" as being cause. We realize that we, ourselves, are cause to our experience. Even though we have people in our experience, the people are really only free to be themselves when we do not worship them or try to possess them.

Love is freedom, Freedom is love. Love releases the people in our lives to their own sufficiency, to their own uniqueness. Love does not demand conformity. Love makes no demands upon anyone and seeks nothing from anyone. Love realizes that one's good is created out of one's own Self. What we believe our Self to be is what we have. What we are now giving is what we are now receiving. Giving is not just some physical gift that you part with on birthdays and at Christmas. Giving is what is continually being expressed. What we are giving to the present moment is what Mind takes and creates as experience. As long as the giving continues, so does the receiving. There is nothing in our experience but what we are now giving. Giving is the sharing of our True Self. All we really have to give is our Self. But that Self is limitless and has within it the resources of the Universe.

We are always dealing with a mental law. It is a law that says, "What I think, believe, feel and express Mind ACCEPTS and ACTS upon. IT ALWAYS CREATES THE FORM AND THE EXPERIENCE OF THAT BELIEF, FEELING AND EXPRESSION." If we are to be free to live fully always, if we are to know health, success, love and prosperity, then we need to put our attention upon WHO and WHAT we REALLY are and not upon what we want from someone else. Our experience is created out of our own thought, out of our own self-expression, not someone else's. If we do not use ideas of greatness, completeness, about our True Self, then Mind can only create the experience of those ideas that we do use, whatever they may be. The people and things in our world are simply shadows of our own consciousness, of our identity, of our Self, for they always respond and correspond to what we are now giving.

A sense of incompleteness, thinking in terms of limitation, causes us to attach ourselves to someone else. We grasp, clutch and try to manipulate others. We are only free, however, when we seek nothing from anyone. Then we are free of fear, anxiety, anger and resentment. We only know health and wealth when we are living out of our Self—when we do not attach ourselves to someone as being cause to our good. When we are about the business of LIVING our True Self, revealing this great and tremendous energy of love that we really are, this absence of need acts upon Mind and Mind fills our life with people and things that represent beauty, love, success and Truth.

Possessions are destructive and negative. Possessions are that which we have to hang on to, that we have to fight to get and fight to keep. They are possessing us. If the things in our life are there easily, lovingly and creatively, they are simply extensions of our consciousness. We use them, enjoy them but are not controlled by them. Things are always in our life in accordance with our level of self-respect and self-esteem. Nothing is worth having if it owns and dominates us. No one is worth having if he or she dictates to us what we must think and what we must do.

If we worry about the things and the people in our world, then they are controlling us and we are not living freely. Our motivation is wrong because we do not feel good enough about our Self. Possessions do not permit us to live completely. "But," you say, "I own a house. It is one of my greatest possessions." But what good is a house if it is controlling us? It is better for us to be our own Self and to let the house be an extension of our Self in which we function. We all demonstrate homes, of all kinds, that reflect our Self. The reality is our own Self. If we are living in a positive, dynamic and creative way, and our house is a means to help us fulfill and express our livingness, that is fine. If, however, we are a slave to that house, always worrying about the mortgage payments, always afraid that someone might spill something, then we are not free. If that house demands all of our free time when we would rather be doing something else, then it is possessing us. If taking care of the house excludes our being involved with our potential and its fulfillment, going to new places and doing new things, then the house owns us and we are not free. We must let the house be an extension of our livingness, our own life-style, and it will be in our life in harmony, balance and perspective.

When we are Self-aware, when we are living fully and completely, we will always have a home that reflects this vital and creative Self. We always have whatever fits our consciousness. It is ours to use. But we must not be bound by it or to it. The more we dare to live and to release into expression the true greatness of our unique Self, the more we will have just those things that are required to help us live freely. We always have whatever we need to express our Self, whatever we believe it to be. In actively acknowledging our completeness, we have no need to overcome anything. Mind takes care of it all. We are no longer fighting shadows. When we are Self-aware, we have no need to get anyone to agree with us. It is only the person who is insecure who needs agreement.

When we love ourselves, there is no need to destroy,

punish, get even, or criticize whoever does not agree with us. Whenever someone tries to force their beliefs upon someone else and to legislate or organize these people, there is going to be conflict. Just as we resent being told what to do if we do not agree, so does someone else resent our doing the same to them. I believe in living a high level of self-esteem. But I cannot make others believe the same thing or make them conform to any of my beliefs.

When we are Self-aware, we are not upset by the actions of others because we realize that they are expressing their own beliefs, their own self-image, whatever it may be. If we are upset by their actions, we are indicating that we believe they have power over us. We are revealing that they have a power to take away or withhold our good. But there is no power outside of our own Self, outside of our beliefs. Our beliefs are shadows of the Mind reflected as our experience. If they are in our life, as person, thing or place, they are there because of the law of our Self. The people in our lives are helping us to fulfill our own beliefs.

The people in our world are there in our experience in terms of what we see them to be. This is really seeing our own Self, our own consciousness and nothing else. If we see dishonesty, cruelty, poverty and disease, we are making an interpretation. We are imposing our Self upon that which is out there, and it is really within our own consciousness. Everything that we see or recognize is within our own Self, otherwise we would not see it, hear it, or recognize it.

Physically fighting someone and using Mind in terms of denial is really the same approach. Trying to overcome either mentally or physically indicates that we are fighting an illusion, something within our Self, a shadow of the Mind. When we believe that we are changing something out there we fail to realize that the change is made first of all in consciousness, which then becomes form. The outer always corresponds to the inner. We can do this in a creative and exciting way. We can begin at the beginning. With the Self. Actively acknowledge what our Ideal Self is. Whatever we can conceive in our thought and put into expression becomes form in our life. When we are really Self-aware there is no need to seek revenge, there is no need to defend ourselves, there is no need to fight the rumors that we hear about ourselves.

When we hear rumors about ourselves we must ask ourselves, why did we hear it? We heard it because we were listening for it through our own consciousness. We always hear what we want to hear. What we fear to hear is really what we want to hear. If we react to it we are saying that this is what we have asked for. If we do not react to it, then we have not really heard it.

There are many times when all sorts of rumors of the world sort of flit by, and we take absolutely no notice of them. The world always has its way of expressing itself. If we do not react to the rumors, then it is not in our consciousness. But if we do, then it couldn't have been accidentally brought to our attention. We have in some way sought it out.

As we are Self-aware and someone disagrees with us, we do not feel a need to defend our Self. We do not get upset by their disagreement. If we do we are not Self-aware. Someone else's disagreement with us is their own self-interpretation and has nothing to do with us. They are experiencing their own consciousness. Too often we are interpreting their actions as a rejection or a contradiction when what they are really saying is "I love you. I think that you are wonderful." Otherwise, why would they be in our life except to say that, and to have it said to them in return? Would they be in our experience at all otherwise? If we are hearing something else, we are hearing an illusion, a shadow of our consciousness, that is not really true.

When we are actively Self-aware, living out the inner idea of life, love, individualized, we do not really have to plan what we are going to say or what we are going to do. This is because the idea with which we are identifying will always tell us what we need to know as we need to know it. .

Have you ever made plans about what you are going to say to someone or what you are going to do about or to someone? If you have, you were dealing with an illusion, for that someone was merely a reflection of something going on within your own consciousness. Those plans were centered on getting rather than giving. They were based upon effect rather than cause.

When we are Self-aware, there is ALWAYS something within our Self that knows what to say, what to give, what to express. As long as we are always BEING our Self, living out of this inner reality, we are divinely guided and given instructions out of that "I" that we are, because Mind always fulfills every concept, every self-image, every idea that we use. First of all we have to be Self-aware.

> "There is One Self, One Presence, One Being. That Self that I really am is God and all that I can conceive of God to be. I am an individualization of It, therefore my good already IS. Since I am that which is forever complete, then mine is the consciousness of Truth, Love, God. I am eternally aware of this Presence living through all that I think, say and do and thus I am free to go anywhere and know infinite success always, for the Presence of God is always in action as me."

When we are actively acknowledging this Presence before we do anything or go anywhere, and keep alive this Presence within our consciousness, then we are

33

always prepared for any challenge that comes along. When ours is the consciousness of love, then greater ideas of loving, of giving, come to us as we require them. When ours is the consciousness of love, then we look beyond every appearance and there is that within us that knows what to say and do to help others awaken to their own sufficiency and beauty. When we are Self-aware, we do not have to treat for guidance over and over again because our active Self-awareness is really our treatment and Mind provides whatever is necessary.

When we are Self-aware, actively knowing Who and What we really are, and we are EXPRESSING the love that we are—our Self-acceptance—then we can only know, express and hear the words of love, which then draw out of the Infinite Mind the action and experience of love. In the active expression of love there are no adversaries. We can only attract into our lives that which we first of all give. That is the law of Mind.

In our Self-awareness, in our Self-expression of this True Self, in believing in our Total Self, if someone should seem to disagree with you, you cannot possibly hear disagreement. You judge not and give them the right to be whatever they are. You are free to go on expressing and experiencing this Self that you accept yourself to BE.

People do certain things. They are all around us going about the business of living out of their own consciousness, being the only thing they can be—themselves. However, if we are sitting in judgment upon them and are reacting with anger to what they are doing, then we cannot see their wholeness, the uniqueness and greatness that is within each and every one. If we react with anger, we have imposed a demand upon them because of our inner insecurity about our own Self, and this is not fair. We are only insecure because we identify with incorrect ideas about our Self. We are imposing a shadow of the mind that has no reality and we are the ones who must suffer. It is always our purpose to look beyond the appearance to see the uniqueness that is really there.

When we plan what we are going to say and do we are dealing with shadows because our plans may not fit the situation when it arrives. It may not be at all what we imagined it was going to be for each moment has its own purpose and its unique opportunities. It is more creative to hang loose, to center our thought on Who and What we really are. It is our purpose to live out of our now Self-acceptance. There is that within each of us that permits us to live spontaneously and It knows exactly what to say, do and give. In rehearsing what SHOULD be done, we are dealing again with a shadow of the Mind. The future is always a shadow and not a reality for all there is is NOW. Planning ahead about how we are going to act takes away from what we are now doing and the way we are now expressing our Self.

We are meant to be out in the world but never OF it. We are meant to move forward in terms of LOVE, COMPLETENESS, TOTALITY, INTEGRITY. If we should walk down a hospital corridor and look into the rooms as we pass by and then react to the appearance, we are dealing with more shadows within our own consciousness. We are not helping either our Self or anyone else. We can be a real blessing as we visit a friend or loved one in a hospital or convalescent home by knowing that perfect life is all there is. As we give the highest of our Self in the present moment, we are giving something to all in our consciousness. Recognizing the perfection and sufficiency of all is a healing action. Sympathy helps no one. Understanding, yes. Sympathy, no. This is because we are then actively accepting some sort of limitation as being a reality. Our worry and sympathy goes into Mind for ourselves and others. Being caught up in a belief in limitation creates the experience of that belief. If we believe that someone else is incomplete, imperfect, this belief can only manifest in our own experience—that is the way the law of Mind works. It is our purpose, wherever we are, wherever we go, to consciously realize that there is only One Power—the Power of Love. The law of Mind is that what we think, believe and express, we must experience. Let us respect this law, not only for our own sake, but for the sake of others.

Our good may seem to come from others, but, in reality, it merely comes through them as a result of our consciousness. Since our consciousness is always cause to our experience, then we are here to build consciousness, to know that the Self that we really are is already complete. We build consciousness by identifying, unifying, with Truth—a great and unlimited idea, and then living that idea. In this way we are a blessing to the world for then wherever we are, order is established, love is expressed, success is known, regardless of who is in our experience.

We always react to what we see and hear, which is within our Self. Our reaction is always our experience. It is very easy to say that we should never react, but if we are reacting, we are believing in a power "out there" and we are thus misinterpreting. What we are reacting to is something within our own Self.

It is our purpose to act, to know Who and What we really are, and to realize that all that goes on around us is like a shadow on the silver screen. This screen simply reflects what we believe our Self to be. When we are busy minding our own business, being involved with the uniqueness of our Total Self, then we are free to act rather than to react. When we are busy giving, there is always action instead of reaction. It is not fair to blame someone else for what happens to us because what we are seeing and hearing is an interpretation of Self. Others are not really doing anything to us at all. When we are actively

Self-aware, when we are involved with Truth about our Self and therefore about everyone else, when we are expressing Love and a sense of completeness, we can only see, hear and experience our True Self. There is really no one else in our experience but our own Self. Everyone in our experience represents a facet of our Self. They are shadows of our Self. The power is Self. There is only one power, one being. Not our Self AND, but our Self AS. Mind is always bringing into our life all that represents our Self-awareness, our level of Self-esteem.

That which is in our life right now is not really all that bad. It may seem to be so by reason of our interpretation. This does not mean that we should ignore the challenges that come along or hide our heads in the sand. Our consciousness must become form. If the environment is to change, there must be change first of all within our consciousness. If our house requires painting, our consciousness of order and beauty must be alive, otherwise we won't even notice. Our consciousness of Truth will always cause Mind to take care of the details so that the house is always in good condition. The house is not cause to our experience. We are. The house is merely an extension of our consciousness. It is a misinterpretation of our Self that permits us to live in poverty, unhappiness, or fear. When we change the way we think about our Self we instantly begin to have a new and different experience. When we are Self-aware, we are no longer upset by what others say and do. Our consciousness of love and order makes sure that love is expressed and experienced, that order becomes visible in every area of our life. Mind cannot say no.

"The power of God is the power of my Self, for there is but One Being, One Self, One Presence, One Power. I am eternally aware of Who and What I really am, which is God uniquely expressed. I am love, order, beauty, life, abundance, power, joy and all that God is. Wherever I go, the law of my Self is drawing into my life opportunities to know and to share this truth of God as me, God as all. Each person who comes into my experience is here as a reflection of my awareness of Truth. I look beyond every seeming appearance. Through the eyes of Self-awareness, I behold the grandeur and greatness of each and every one."

CHAPTER II

Stand on Principle

Principle is one of the great lessons we must learn if we are to be free of the shadows of the Mind. The law of our Being is always in action, it is always creating in terms of our Being. The law can never be denied or circumvented. Principle is more than just the law of mind. It is a conscious use of that law, but always at the level of our highest Self. It is always used by means of Truth. We can talk about all of our problems to everyone who comes to us and we will maintain those problems simply because we are activating them by our attention. Since they are our point of attention, Mind must maintain them. We often try to use Principle, failing to realize that we are not at one with Truth. We do this often when we apply the science of Mind in order to get something, to treat for acquiring something. We are not using Principle when we try to heal the body or to demonstrate the right mate. This is because our use of mind is based upon the idea that we are not already complete.

If we are to stand on Principle, we must not search for ways to use Spiritual Power. We must let that Spiritual Power use us. When we seem to need something, that something is not what we really need.

What we really require is the realization of Who and What we truly are. When we have that realization we are eternally standing on Principle for we are always aware that we are already whole, perfect and complete. We are standing on Principle only when we are actively revealing the sufficiency that is the truth of our nature. We are standing on Principle when we treat others as if they are mature and unique individualizations of God. We are not standing on Principle when we give in to others and do their work for them or shoulder their responsibilities.

Our Self has work to do. Our Self has sufficiency to live and to prove. And so does the Self of each person in our life. Mothers who think that they are being loving by catering to the whims of their children and wind up doing their work for them are not only not standing on Principle, they are directing the law of Mind to keep their children immature rather than help them unfold as self-sufficient adults.

Mind is everywhere present and so the law of our Self is in action regardless of where we are. Someone told me recently that when she heard that a friend of hers was in the hospital and that no visitors were allowed, she went there anyway and just sat in the lobby praying for that person to pull through. There is nothing wrong in going to the hospital to do that if you are so guided, but Truth can be known regardless of where you are. Our presence in the hospital is not necessary because Mind is everywhere present and what we know where we are is known everywhere.

Principle is the realization that each and every person is an active channel through which God reveals Itself. To teach our children that they do not have a part to play in life is against principle. To teach them that they are unique, intelligent, and self-sufficient is Principle. To be worried or concerned about our friends is also against Principle. If we know that God is the ONLY power, then God is all there is and there is nothing to be concerned about. Worry is a denial of God.

When we seek to be rid of our problem we are working against Principle because we are then trying to overcome something. We are saying that we believe in two powers rather than one. There is nothing to overcome when we believe that God is all there is. This does not mean that we sit around and do nothing. It means, instead, that we are actively revealing our sufficiency, that we are consciously knowing the Truth and are living it. Stand on Principle and let it work. Mind can only create that which corresponds to what we are giving. When we try to get we are chasing away our good. When we try to make something happen we are living a belief that our good is not already so.

We are standing on Principle when we are outgoing, expressing love for the sake of expressing love, no matter who is in the picture. Keep in mind that love is not sex. When we are out socially we are working against Principle if we expect someone to come over and woo us. We are right on Principle when we reach out and express our Whole Self regardless of whether someone rejects us or not. Let go of the desire to get rid of the problem and instead face the challenge at hand without fear by daring to be your True Self.

When we seek to get someone else to pay our bills we are completely against Principle for we are then denying our own ability to be self-sufficient. Someone may come along and give us something or even pay some of those bills as a result of our own expression of sufficiency, but if we are hinting, begging, or conniving, that is not Principle at all. That is looking outside of our Self for our good and in doing that something will be taken from us instead. We are not here to demonstrate our good at the expense of someone else. What we need to do is to demonstrate our own good and this can be done only by our standing on Principle every step of the way.

Someone asked me what to do about all of the chain letters that they receive. Usually that type of letter includes a warning that you must send copies of that letter to four or five others within a certain time. If you do not, the letter says, you will have seven years of bad luck or bring great disaster to yourself and possibly your whole family. Many let this idea be a shadow in their mind and are controlled by it. If they do not do as the letter says, they begin to look for disaster to strike—and, sure enough, it does. Whatever we look for we find. I have received letters like that also, but I simply release them, knowing that they have nothing to do with me. If I am standing on Principle, forever being Self-aware, then I know that nothing can touch me except that which reflects my Self. I am not cause to anyone else's good or problem, nor is anyone else cause to mine. A letter is not cause to anything. The cause to my now experience is the idea that I have chosen to live. When we choose to stand on Principle, then that choice or that decision has the intelligence of the Universe that guides and directs our way in the fulfillment of that choice.

"I am dedicated to Principle, to living and revealing the power of love now and always." As we go our own way, letting that idea use us, Mind can do nothing else but create out of that idea. Principle means that we are already whole and that wholeness is now the Truth of all in our world, for Mind is everywhere present. When we stand on Principle we are free to move forward as the action of completeness in every area of our life.

As we enter into the pathway of true freedom, prosperity, love and health, as we begin to live the Presence of Love, there are sometimes physical and mental upheavals that appear to challenge us and we become mystified. We think that perhaps we are going in the wrong direction. However, these upheavals are there because up to this point we have based our peace of mind, harmony and good upon the material aspects of law and order. We have looked for our good from someone else.

It is true that our point of attention is always our experience and that when we are expressing Love, we are no longer dealing with shadows of the mind the outer picture changes to correspond. But often it takes some kind of upheaval, demonstrated out of our own consciousness, to cause us to really look within, to really dedicate ourselves to Truth rather than to our dependence upon people and things.

Even as we move along the spiritual path there have got to be new and greater challenges. Otherwise we begin to die. Even Spirit seeks to experience more of Itself in new and greater ways. Who wants to live in the Garden of Eden, in a state of pure bliss but always on the same level, throughout eternity? We would not grow and we would soon be bored to tears. We need to ever be moving forward, and this does not happen when everything stays the same.

When you begin to stand on Principle, things automatically begin to happen. They are all for the better even though they seem to shake the very foundations of your way of life. If upheaval causes you to be more completely Self-aware, then it has fulfilled its purpose. If that upheaval frees you from the authority of someone else, then it has been necessary. The law of your Being has demanded that change and has gotten it. There is good that comes out of every challenge. When you have chosen the pathway of Self-awareness and are using Principle, things are never going to be the same. Since we resist change at the human level, that change will be interpreted as bad or unnecessary if our attention strays from Who and What we really are. Let us say, then, that upheaval is our letting go of looking to anyone or any thing for our good. It is our now dependence upon Principle, upon God, and nothing else. We are always the experience of our Self, our consciousness, our Self-expression, and we cannot experience anything unless we have chosen it or are ready for it. If we see that upheaval is negative, it is because we have gone back to our dependence upon person, place and thing rather than upon Principle.

There have been those who have hit rock bottom before they were forced to turn within, before they chose to change their way of life. But they came to that decision, to move beyond their present way of life, and probably would not have made that decision without having "hit the gutter," so to speak. That upheaval was then a great blessing.

I believe that all upheaval is a blessing. I believe that it is the law of our Being creating a divine opportunity to stand on Principle, to be more completely Self-aware, and out of all of this comes a new and greater way of life. There is within each of us the ability to go through any and every challenge. We do not know that we have this ability until we go through it, however.

Never run away from any challenge for that is never the pathway of self-discovery. I am not saying that we each of us have individually caused shortages or prices to climb or that we have caused endless snow-falls or inclement weather. These are still opportunities to know that there is that within us that has a special and unique answer to every challenge. Challenges are always opportunities to test our self-sufficiency, to permit an inner Intelligence to come through us to give us our special answer.

When we sit and wait for our answer to come to us, we never have it. We experience that answer only as we move, as we express. The answer comes out of the action, the expression of our belief in our Self. Some say that they are waiting for the "Will of God" to be revealed before they do anything, but in doing that they have closed their consciousness to the answers of God. God's answer can only come forth as we are revealing the Presence of God. Yes, THY WILL BE DONE, by all means. But how can we know what THY WILL is until we are living the idea, "God as me?" We are ready for our experience only as we experience it, as we express it. The upheaval may be the way consciousness provides in order for us to get moving. When great demands are made upon us, we become truly alive. As we move out to face these demands, the answers arrive. They are in the NOW, in the ACTION, in the demand that we are making upon our potential, upon our inner True Self.

Patterns are being changed when we no longer are depending upon the laws of the land to provide our good, to protect us and to show us the way. When we are standing on Principle, the law of the Self is the law of God, and we are living as greatness, as the genius that each of us really is. When we choose to live the genius of our True Self, things begin to hum, pop and crackle. Sometimes it seems as though all "hell" were breaking loose, but what it really is, is our daring to be our own Self. We are living the uniqueness of our Self, we are outgoing, dynamic, assertive expressions of love, life, prosperity and wholeness. This type of personality always generates, makes waves, causes things to happen.

So many people feel that life is passing them by only because they are waiting for something to happen. When they choose to live, then things really begin to happen. We do not use the Science of Mind in order to live in the same old way. No indeed. We are here to let Principle stir things up.

When we demonstrate a new and better job, we do not do so with the idea that there is going to be less work, less responsibility, less action. The greater job may bring with it more work, more responsibility and more action. And certainly more challenges. Our higher level of consciousness, of Self-awareness, acts upon Mind and Mind creates upheavals, challenges and opportunities. That is all a part of this way of life—Self-discovery.

We can know peace of mind and serenity while we are in the thick of things, while we are very much in the world, living in an exciting and positive way. We do this when we believe in our Self, when we know that Mind is taking care of the details while we live the uniqueness of our Self. When we know that we are ready for any and every challenge that comes along.

When we are standing on Principle, it is the Truth that is embodied within our consciousness that is the power of our life, not some one. Without the consciousness of Truth, we are absolutely nothing. We may think that we have an edge on other people because we have connections, because we happen to know some influential people. And so we ask favors, counting on those certain people to pull certain strings and thus get for us whatever it is that we desire. But in counting on those people, we are dependent upon their moods, their seeking a return favor, their own problems and their degree of influence. In counting on someone else, we are always on shaky ground. It is not Who you know that counts, but WHAT you are KNOWING and WHAT you are LIVING.

It seems to be the American dream to demonstrate great wealth and riches without really doing anything for it. We dream of someone leaving us a great fortune in their will. Or, it might be that in some way we know the right person and he provides for us an executive position where all we have to do is spend an unlimited expense account while doing very little work. We dream of owning the mansion that somehow appears from out of nowhere and is ours to live in forever, gratis. It never works out that way. We have to earn our good by right of consciousness in order for it to be attained and maintained.

It is not because we may be a practitioner that any healing takes place. It is not because we may be a minister or belong to a certain church that great miracles seem to happen. No. All of this happens only when we are living the Truth. It is not only the Truth that sets us free but the LIVING OF THAT TRUTH. Truth is that which has be be individually lived and expressed for it is only what we are living that counts, that directs Mind.

We may know the right people because we are living the Truth, and they may seem to help us, but all the while it is simply the Truth, that we have directed into subconsciousness Mind that is taking care of the details.

So many children of famous and successful people have so many problems and get into so much trouble. Why? It is because they have not been taught by their parents that each and every one has to earn their own good. Each of us must stand on Principle for ourselves. It is the only way we can build a high level of self-esteem. No one else can do this for us.

Going to the practitioner, the counselor, the psychologist, is but a temporary measure, for he or she can know the Truth and help us go through the challenge at hand, but they cannot be with us forever. Neither can Mom and Dad.

Children cannot depend upon their parents, nor can they really depend upon their teachers. Teachers have as their responsibility pointing the way for all of their students to stand on their own two feet. It is always what we ourselves are knowing and living today that is directing the law of Mind for our Self. It is always what WE know and what WE are living that directs Mind—not Who we know.

We may know some celebrity or some great teacher, and knowing them can be an honor and a privilege, but these friendships do not necessarily mean that we are free to live fully and completely at all times. It is what we ourselves individually know and do that counts.

Many famous entertainment figures are surrounded by their entourage or hangers-on. The hangers-on feel a certain sense of pride and pleasure simply because they are seen with someone who is famous. But the hanger-on is just a face in the background. He is in the shadows. He is not earning his own good, living his own life, doing his own thing, and so his own life is not very meaningful or fulfilling.

There are many people who pay a few dollars and become a licensed and ordained minister. That does not mean that they are a blessing to the world. That does not mean that they are helping people awaken to their own potential. It may be a way of avoiding paying taxes, or an ego-booster, but unless they are living the Truth at all times they are not really ordained. So many people start out in the ministry, having visions of saving the world or to become famous as a great speaker or healer. The title does not heal. The title may impress certain people, but robes and titles do not heal nor do they a minister make.

So many people have the mistaken idea that their practitioner can pray for them and then all they have to do is to wait for their good to appear. If the practitioner is treating and knowing the Truth, then it is the practioner who demonstrates his good. He prays for the purpose of bringing alive within the consciousness of his client the Truth, so that the patient then moves out and lives and expresses that Truth. Truth is always an individual experience. Success is an individual experience which cannot be given to us by anyone. Everything is an individual experience.

So many people become discouraged, waiting, waiting, waiting for their good to appear. They fail to realize that their good is what they are now giving, sharing and revealing. The receiving is automatic. That is the way the creative power of Mind works. We can know the President of the United States and still be a failure. We can know the producer of movies and still not know how to act. We have all been aware of certain people who have been pushed into so-called stardom by the "right people" only to fail because they were not producing something or generating anything of their own.

Body begins to reflect perfection as long as perfection is acknowledged and expressed. Our finances begin to be in divine order only when we ourselves are living and expressing abundance. The attitude and state of mind must be established and maintained. We do this by living a great idea. Others can help us, yes, but our own receptivity to the Truth is imperative. Many people ask me to treat for their husbands, wives. All the while they know the people for whom the requests are being made do not believe in the Truth or Principle and would not want anyone praying for them.

Consciousness may very well bring someone of influence into the picture. They may be a part of the manifestation. But the cause is always the Truth that we ourselves are individually knowing, living and expressing. The law of our Being is always fulfilled. Get busy today and live the Truth yourself if you desire to be free.

There is nowwhere in the world a prison that could possibly equal that of our own consciousness when it is filled with hate, anger, envy, jealousy, resentment, all of which add up to fear. Fear is the result of trying to get rather than to give. It is the result of not standing on Principle. It is a result, possibly, of using Mind at the mental level rather than at the Spiritual. Spirit is our conscious Self-awareness at the level of God. Fear is believing that our good is "out there" and that someone can either give it to us or take it away.

Even though fear is not created out of reality, it still imprisons us. It keeps us from going out into the world and actively, lovingly communicating.

A fear of being rejected enslaves us so that we do not even make the attempt to communicate. A fear of being judged keeps us from even trying. Since we only have what we give, when we are not giving, we are not living. We have nothing when we are not reaching out to share.

Many people feel that the worst possible experience is to be alone. It is this fear that enslaves them. They desperately try to attach themselves to others, only to drive them away.

The fear of growing old alone causes many people to marry someone whom they do not really like. It causes them to bribe or to support others, thereby taking away the sufficiency and the joy of self-discovery from those to whom they attach themselves.

There are those who have an obsessive fear of germs and do everything possible to protect themselves from these demons. But germs have no power over anything or anyone. Germs are to us what we are to ourselves. Some people seal themselves into their homes or their rooms for fear of being contaminated. But it is this fear that errupts within in one way or another and so they have not escaped the idea that is alive within their consciousness. What we fear ever comes upon us for we are literally asking for that fear to come true for us.

A woman whose husband left her for another woman entered into an affair in which she desperately clung to her lover for fear that he would escape. Only by having someone with her did she feel at all acceptable. Yet this fear of being alone, of being rejected, caused her lover to leave her. She felt "dumped" and was having a hard time facing herself. She had used mental treatment in order to bring this man into her life and it had backfired. Using mental treatment to get something or someone causes us to be controlled by what we are trying to get. We must stand on Principle and recognize that we are already complete. When it is our purpose to give, not to get, the law of our Being easily attracts othes into our lives and permits them to stay with ease.

Love holds no one in bondage. When we are expressing love, we not only release the people in our world to their own uniqueness, but we help to release them from their own prisons of fear. We are free of fear when we realize that the law of our being is always in action and is forever bringing to us all that our self-expression represents. When we actively acknowledge our completeness we no longer seek our good from anyone and we are automatically free of fear. Realize that the law of our Self must attract into our life whoever represents that Self that we are expressing and we will never be alone.

Every limiting thought that we use about ourselves or others is really a prison. We are controlled by the thought. Mind always finds the way to create an experience of that thought. Mind always creates the form of all that we are thinking and feeling. Even those thoughts that we apply to others have power in our own experience. If we make judgments and see others as either being good, bad, sick, well, rich or poor, negative or positive, we are holding them in bondage, the prisoners of those beliefs. Our judgment, whatever it is, is a shadow of the Mind and we are controlled by it. When we let go of the judgment and begin minding our own business there is no fear, there is no prison.

Since Mind is eternally creating the forms of fear, we must find a way to transcend fear. Fear manifests as physical limitations and thus limits our free-flowing expression of life. Our bodies always reflect what we feel. Joy produces health while fear produces disease. The only way to know and experience joy is to give up our desires to get and our expectations of what others can or should give us. In praying for the right mate we too often do it with the motivation of having someone to take care of us. Prayer for the purpose of getting is the way to loneliness and fear.

When we have a high level of Self-esteem and choose to acknowledge our sufficiency we no longer have a need to get. When we have attained Self-awareness, Self-acceptance, Mind is free to attract to us whoever represents the love that we are now able to express. We can express love only when we love ourselves and we can only love ourselves when we are accomplishing, giving, Being.

There are those who stay at home and never go anywhere because they have a fear of driving. They only go somewhere when there is someone available to drive them. They are thus in prison. The fear of driving is simply a result of not trusting the Self, which is really God. It is believing that someone can do something to us. No one can ever do anything to us. They simply help us fulfill our beliefs. When we regard ourselves as being insufficient we do not trust our Self and we are controlled by a shadow of the Mind.

Fear is directed to what or what might not happen. When we live in the now and dare to express our True Self, there is no referral to what has already happened or to what might take place. When we direct our attention to Who and What we really are we are free to live in an exciting and adventurous way. We must love ourselves. We must dare to trust this Self that is all-intelligent and all-knowing. Only by living out of our Self, standing on the Principle of "God-as-me" can we really live and really give.

When we believe that there is nothing that we can do about the challenge at hand, then we are bound by that idea. We are being controlled by this shadow as long as we believe it, as long as this belief is using us. There is always something that we can do. However, if we believe that we are overcoming a problem rather than fulfilling our purpose of giving, we are still controlled by what we are trying to overcome. We must use the idea that we are expressing success, love, joy, health and all that we desire, that we are revealing our self-sufficiency, rather than trying to overcome something.

If ours is the challenge of not being able to communicate or to express love, our purpose is, use our thought to arrive at Self-love and then shower that love upon all regardless of where we are. There is always something that we can do to show love. What we are expressing always reveals our intent and Mind can only create out of this intent. When we are standing on Principle, we are expressing and revealing the Presence of God, which is love, and we are not trying to overcome anything. There is always something that we can give to the present moment as love.

So many people say that their lives are uninteresting, drab and dull because their situation does not permit them to do adventurous things. They live quiet and passive lives because that represents their self-image. They are waiting for Prince Charming or Miss America to come along and whisk them away into a life of excitement, beauty and love. They are looking outside of their Self for the excitement and joy of living. The only place to find these qualities are within our own Self.

If we are not satisfied with our life situation as it stands right now, we ourselves must do something about it. We do something about it by actively identifying with our Total Self. Pour enthusiasm into every action. Make a choice to be adventurous and vital and fully alive. We must do this every day, every moment.

So many people do not move into action because they are afraid of making a mistake, Making a mistake to them is the worst thing that could possibly happen. But there is no shame in making a mistake. Every successful person has made loads of them. If we are afraid to experiment, we are afraid to live. If we are afraid to live, then we are afraid of dying and are thus dying every day. If we want a certain life style, we must begin to express it from this moment on. Mind gives us the answers as we go along, but Mind needs to know our intent. It needs to know what we are all about.

Someone wrote to me telling me of her challenge of living in a small midwestern town which simply did not permit her to live the way that she wanted to live. She felt that her life style of her Ideal Self could only be fulfilled in either San Francisco, New York City, Los Angeles, Chicago or Paris. She had money but felt that if she went to San Francisco, it might turn out to be the wrong place. The place really has nothing to do with it. You experience your Self wherever you are. She was afraid to make a mistake, to experiment. The right place is always where we are living as long as we are revealing our True Self. We can express our ideal qualities no matter what the location. We are not suddenly going to be living our Ideal when we get to where we are going. We have got to be doing it where we are right now.

It is true that our life styles demand certain environments, but these are always demonstrated out of "life-style," out of "Self-action," not the other way around. Consciousness always becomes form, whether it be body, job, mate or city.

We must not be afraid to experiment. We must not be afraid to make a mistake. We have learned from our mistakes more than from anything else. Living greatly requires that we take chances.

Many people are attracted to the Science of Mind because they believe it will keep them from making mistakes. However, there are lessons that we all have to learn and a certain action must be considered going through what we need to in order to learn what we need to know. In daring to be our Self, in daring to take chances, in daring to be the action of our True Self, we can never really make a mistake. The demonstration is the action, not the result.

When we learn to develop the habit of action rather than passivity things begin to happen and life is not dull. There is something within each of us that knows what to do, what action to take, what to give. We must stop dealing with what might or might not happen and put our attention on expressing those qualities that we choose to experience.

We will never find our right answer by doing nothing. Waiting for our answer before we move forth only assures us that we will never make a move. We never really reach "the top," but it is in reaching for the top that keeps us going, and it is our going forward that directs Mind to create accordingly. We must let Self-action be our goal rather than getting some thing. We must let communication be our purpose rather than getting a proposal of marriage. We always demonstrate the forms of our Self-action. We can never make a mistake when we are reaching out and expressing love.

We can never make a mistake when we dare to be our

True Self. So what if someone does not agree or seem to want what we are giving? It is this Self-action that counts. It is this expression of our inner greatness that is directing Mind so that Mind can create accordingly.

Our desire to get is our only mistake. Our need to be accepted and approved is our only mistake. Self-action is the way. The answer always comes out of the now action that is taking place through us and in this action of moving forward there is no fear, there is no problem, there is only our potential.

Every challenge demands action on our part. If there is no activity, the person who faces the challenge is very seriously crippled because it is our action that directs Mind and teaches us what we need to know. Prayer or treatment is not for the purpose of getting something or making something happen, but to bring each of us to the point of action. Anything that stands in the way of positive, creative and dynamic action makes us a prisoner. The thing that causes us to move forward is our own unification with the Presence, our True Self. We do not move if we do not believe in ourselves. It is our Self-action that causes us to be free of fear.

It is not only our responsibility to act ourselves, but to help others to arrive at the point where they are in action as well. When we are announcing to the world and to the law of Mind Who and What we are, the world automatically cooperates. This is the way that Mind works. The world is always a reaction to what we are first of all giving out.

If we are bullies, the world may not like it, but at least it knows what to do about us. It gives back what we are giving out. If we are lovers, then the world responds accordingly because it now knows that what we are all about is love and so it gives back love. It cannot help doing so. If we give nothing, then we receive nothing. If we are a passive non-participant in life, then that is

56

the signal for the world to take over and control us. In doing nothing we are literally ·directing Mind to bring into our life someone to take charge of us, to rule our lives.

We are either active or non-active. If we are active, we believe in our own Self. We love and respect our Self. If we are passive, then we do not believe in our Self and we are in some way saying that we do not believe in God. The law of life is, that we only have what we are now expressing.

We should develop a high degree of Self-action. We should do whatever we can to maintain that degree of activity. We are not here to be entertained. We are here to act. Also, when we live out of self-initiative, we can only maintain that self-actualization by not trying to influence others. Whatever or whoever we are trying to influence is controlling us because we see him or her or it as a power outside of our Self, a power that can either give or withhold.

No matter what the situation, the people in our life really desire to be self-sufficient and self-reliant. They cannot be this if we are always doing their work for them, if we are trying to do their thinking for them. There is certainly nothing wrong in teaching our children the law of mathematics in helping him or her with their homework. But if we do it for them, they are not discovering their own Self-worth. They are then not aware that there is an intelligence within them that can do anything. We are then teaching them to be passive rather than to be active. If we believe that the way to handle them is to do their work for them so that there can be peace around the house, then we are making a statement about our own Self rather than about them.

There is power in the activity of daring to be our own Self. There is power of learning to live out of our own Self-initiative. Waiting for something to happen merely means that we are directing Mind to wait. Forcing something to happen is trying to get in a dynamic way and it always backfires. Self-action is going within for our own unique answer and then moving into the action of our True, Ideal, God-Self.

We maintain Self-initiative by expressing our Self regardless of what the world thinks, whether it agrees with us or not. In looking for a reaction from the people in our world we are being influenced by them rather than letting the world be influenced by us.

Synergy is the exciting result of two whole individuals each giving of their unique talents, energies, enthusiasm and Inner greatness to a common purpose. We can certainly do things with others, but Self-initiative does not try to influence. Synergy supports totally the sufficiency of not only our own Self, but the Self of our partner as well. We each have a part to play. Self-initiative does not demand that the other agree with us. It does not demand that we have our way and that someone else give in. It means that we have within our Self something special to give and we are proud of the way that our potential is working through us. Because we are doing this, others are influenced to do the same.

Each person has his own activity that must be expressed. When we bring in the idea of self-sufficiency we do not mean that we are going to eliminate people from our life. Quite the contrary. The law of our Being is always in action and draws to us whoever represents whatever it is that we are expressing. We can never get away from the results of our now action. But in hoping, wishing, and needing someone to be by our side always reveals that we are trying to get rather than to give. We do not need to be alone but we will always be lonely when we are trying to find someone who will understand us. Since we are all on different levels of consciousness and since no two people are alike, we can never find someone who really understands what we are completely all about.

It seems to be a paradox, but in order to have people in our life creatively, we must release them and we must live out of our own Self-initiative. The more we look outside of our Self, the more lonely we are. The more we try to find someone to make us happy, the less chance we have of finding the ideal. The more that we are involved with our own activity, the more that action draws to us whoever and whatever represents that action.

When we stand on Principle we are living out of our own Self. We are interpreting everything through our True Self and what we see and hear is good. When we look outside of our Self for our good, we must plot, scheme and use other people in order to attain our goals.

Cancer is often the result of trying to make something happen. Even in trying to be healed of cancer one is trying to make something happen. The Science of Mind can be used to heal and it does work, even though it proves to be temporary. The outer world, which includes our bodies, is merely a corresponding equivalent to our now invisible level of Self-awareness. If we are forever watching body, then we are putting power into our belief in body as cause, and body is result. Our healing is only temporary because we do not work to attain and maintain a consciousness of love. Our every effort to heal is directed at something separate and apart from Truth, from Life, from God. If we acknowledge that God is the only power, then we know that there is nothing to heal. Treatment or prayer must not be for the purpose of healing God. It is for the purpose of being aware of that which we already are.

When we fall in love romantically we often feel that we want to know every single detail about the object of our love. But the more "facts" we learn, the less we really know of them. The more facts we gather about them, the less they become the ideal. The same is true

59

of our political leaders. The more we know about what they have done or not done, the less ideal they become. We then become disenchanted and vote them out of office. The Reality of each person has nothing to do with the facts and figures in their biographies. The Reality is invisible. The Reality is, that each and every one is an individualization of God.

The more we put our attention on body the less we learn. The more we go after something, the less we have. It is the Truth that sets us free, not the outlining of what we want to have happen.

Every time that we treat for health we are not standing on Principle. We are then trying to heal God and God is already complete, already perfect. We are then trying to heal our Self, and God is already the nature of our Self.

In treating for money we are out of Principle because we are saying that we need, that we are experiencing poverty and lack. We are looking at form, and form can do nothing. Effects have no power, yet our belief in its power enslaves us. We are once more dealing with the shadows of the mind.

We are advised by some psychologists that we must become optimists if we are to live fully. In order to be an optimist we must stop watching the world. We must cease listening to the facts and figures that are presented to us. We must stand on Principle.

It is only when we are free of what is going to happen that we have the optimistic state of mind. It is always when we are trying to get that we have depression. The more we try to get, the more we have to try to use others. The more that we use others, the more they are controlling us. In being controlled we are automatically depressed.

Truth needs no healing. Life needs no healing. God

needs no healing. As we acknowledge the ALL, the WHOLE, It takes over and lives through our consciousness.

We see example after example in life of those who try to rise to the top of the heap through their machinations, through their burning need to be in a position of power. But all of us are in positions of power, greater power than we can realize, simply by letting go of getting and seeing our goal as one of expressing and revealing the Presence of God through all that we do. In being the optimist, we have greater power to use for we are now letting the Law take care of the details while we direct it through Self-awareness.

The more we worship body, the more body becomes imperfect. The more we try to make something happen, the more the law seems to backfire. But God simply does not need to be healed or changed. God already is full, It is forever complete. Even as we acknowledge this Presence It may guide us to do something, to go to a doctor, to eat in a certain way, but It is guiding us out of that completeness that It is, and consciousness now becomes form as guidance, as this inner direction.

Mind not only creates, It gives to us out of Itself what we need to know in order to fulfill each and every state of mind, way of thought, or self-image. Stand on Principle. Acknowledge that you are created in the image and likeness of God...that you are already complete. Nothing can take away your good. It already is. We can only demonstrate and have that which is equivalent to what we believe our Self to be.

"Since I am created out of the Mind of God so that God might express and experience Itself by means of me, then all that God is I already am. I am that which is forever whole and complete. I am the health, wealth, love and success that God already is. My every thought is directed to this wholeness that I forever am, this Presence of God as me. I am free of the temptation to demonstrate person, place and thing for I know that I am Life, which is God, and in the Life of the wholeness that I forever live are all of the forms that represent my capacity to express the life of God. I know that all forms are an instantaneous and automatic reaction to the Life which God lives as me.

"Regardless of what others do or say, I am free of the temptation to look at and accept the appearance as a reality. I know and believe that God is all there is, and since I live in the consciousness of God, then my dedication to Principle keeps me forever free of being tempted by the voices of the world.

"I live the Invisible, which cannot help but become visible. This invisible Presence of God that I forever express is the center of my attention. I am not fooled by any bid for attention from the world. I live the Presence and thus I am Life. Life is the substance of all that is in my world, for it is my purpose always to live each moment to the fullest, permitting consciousness to become form in terms of Itself."

CHAPTER III

Assume the Responsibility

There is not a single problem or challenge in our whole life that cannot be met and gone through by means of being our own Self, our Total Self. It is only because we are not completly Self-aware that there seems to be a problem.

If we find ourselves reacting in any way to what others are doing or are saying, this tells us that we are not Self-aware. This reveals that we believe that the power in our life is outside rather than within. We cannot and must not run away from the challenge. Just as we can never run away from ourselves, for the challenge is only our Self becoming form. Whenever we find ourselves reacting, assume the responsibility...know that we must do something about our own patterns of thought rather than doing something about someone else.

Too many people are still trying to do something about someone else. They are trying to reform, to change or even heal others. But whatever we see is within our own Self. It is our responsibility to know and to live the Truth, to acknowledge Who and What we really are, right then and there. The Truth is that there is nothing but Love. This responsiblity is ours. Saying to ourselves that we will take care of the challenge tomorrow is not assuming the responsibility. If the challenge comes to us, then it is our own responsibility, no one elses.

We must work on ourselves always to be free of all boundaries, opinions, judgments and memories of previous experience. If some problem has come to us, we must know that our Self has drawn this opportunity to us.

The idea that is alive within our consciousness is what we always experience, regardless of whether that idea seems to be about someone else or not. It is the consciousness of sufficiency, love, health, wealth and completeness that creates freedom, independency, then interdependency, and love, and no one can do this for us.

As a result of the changes in consciousness of people today the idea of self-sufficiency is coming more and more alive. As a result of the changing moral climate, and ways of life, more and more women realize that they cannot depend upon their husbands for their security or their eternal good. Many people unceremoniously depart for the next phase of life (make their transition), leaving loved ones behind ill-prepared to take care of themselves. Many "leave the nest" because they are seeking their happiness from someone else.

The changing sense of responsibility in the world points out to us that we ourselves have to assume the responsibility for our own livelihood, our own happiness, our own health, our own sense of security. Now that we know that Mind creates our every experience we realize even more that our entire experience is created out of our Self-image and that we cannot look to anyone else for our good.

It is only when we live out of our own consciousness of sufficiency that we draw to us others who help fulfill that sufficiency. This is the law of attraction. It is only when we are expressing our own sufficiency that we demand that others do the same and thus not lean or depend upon us. The power in our life is within our own Self, and the more that we cease looking to others, except for sharing, the more freely and completely we are going to live.

Every belief that comes to our attention has to be met within our own consciousness. This is our responsibility. If we do not take charge, we are going to accept this opinion of someone else as being a truth and we are then going to experience it ourself in some way.

Someone asked me recently, "What do you do about someone you know who is ill?" If you know that they are ill, then you are accepting the belief in illness. In essence you are saying that you do not believe in God. It is our responsibility in helping them to actively acknowledge that God is the only Power—to affirm that perfection, immortality, completeness, are the only Reality. It is our responsibility to speak to the WHOLENESS of the person who is living out of a sense of separation or a belief in incompleteness. Every claim must be met with the Truth that we ourselves are already living. If we find ourselves not living it, then we must get busy and do exactly that. It is the only way we can help others.

Our reaction of fear, if that should be the case, merely indicates that we do not believe in our Self, this individualization of God that we really are.

There is not God AND disease. There is not God AND poverty. There is only God. God precludes anything else. If we believe in God—that Allness, Wholeness and Perfection that is everywhere present—then we are acknowledging that WHOLENESS within every situation, every condition, every experience. What appears to be is but a shadow of the mind.

Do not give this responsibility to someone else for it

is what we ourselves are knowing that counts. It is what we ourselves are feeling that counts. It is what we are expressing that is directing Mind to create our OWN experience.

The law of our Self is always attracting to us whoever and whatever represents our Self. The law of our Self is always creating opportunities for us to prove our belief in this Self. Just because we are denying the negative and affirming the positive does not mean that we will never have another problem. As a matter of fact, our denying of the negative and affirming the positive means that we believe in a power outside of our Self. We are affirming a belief in God AND, and this is an impossibility. Our belief must then become form.

For every claim that comes to us that causes us to see limitation, there is a responsibility to do something about our Self. We are the leader in our life. We are the power. We can never change someone else. We can only change the way we are thinking about our own Self, which then changes the way we think about others. Every person in our life represents something within our own consciousness. Each is a shadow of the mind.

Actively identify with the ideal of God as Me, God as all. Let that ideal be revealed through all that we think, say and do. It is this ideal that goes before us by means of Mind, attracting to us Its own. Assume the responsibility of living out of this Ideal. Dare to express your belief in this Ideal. Dare to assume the responsibility of living this Ideal. No one can do this for us.

The people who love us today may not feel the same way tomorrow. The people who are with us today may be gone tomorrow. It is not because we are forcing them out of our lives. Their own consciousness recreates itself, as does ours. So...let our life represent us at our highest.

Assume the responsibility of letting go of person, place

and thing, and contact the inner Ideal. No longer try to relate the Kingdom of God to the disease, the problem or the condition. So much of prayer fails because it tries to bring God down to the problem, and God cannot be influenced to know other than Its own perfection. God does not even know what a problem is. It is not interested in anyone's problem. Only the solution. If God had concepts of limitation within Its own consciousness, those concepts would no longer permit It to be God.

God is that which is forever Whole and Complete. Completeness cannot be aware of incompleteness.

Begging God to help us out is directing Mind at the level of incompleteness and it is the belief in incompleteness that causes Mind to create accordingly.

If there is a problem and we are trying to free ourselves of that problem, the problem is still our point of attention. In treating to be free of it, we are still emphasizing the problem. It is a contradiction to acknowledge God as the only power and then try to get God to handle the problem. God does not know what a problem is. So the prayer seems to fail and we get discouraged. We blame God for not listening to us. But how can God listen, when God can hear only the voice of success, beauty, abundance, completeness—which is the voice of Itself? It is only "I Am" ideas that heal, if those "I Am" ideas reveal the nature of God.

We can only experience what we can understand. We can only understand what we are.

Whatever we try to change, even in the way of prayer, is our point of attention. It must then be maintained in our life. Why? Because Mind can only create in terms of our way of thought, our way of expression. Since most prayer is for the purpose of getting something, then that consciousness that needs, that is trying to add to itself, must be maintained. God cannot be influenced to do anything. God is a way of thought. It can only go on doing what It is doing. It can only go on giving and revealing Itself. We must surrender this need, this desire, to get what we want by changing the world. We must let go of trying to get something, and we must acknowledge that we are already complete.

You only have what you reveal and so as we begin to use our thought simply to be Self-aware, we use our thought to acknowledge the Kingdom of God within. We begin to pour out into expression the integrity of our True Self. We begin to give to the moment, to others, with non-attachment. We begin to express out of our God-being. We begin to individualize God.

The alcoholic does not have the challenge of overcoming his need to drink, to run away, or to punish himself. What he does have is the opportunity to reveal the Presence of God. He has the responsibility of expressing his God-Self in all that he does. When his attention is upon giving the highest of his Self, his integrity, that is what he does give. He is not praying to be saved. In his prayer he is instead acknowledging that it is the Father within that doeth the work. He is using his thought to center on the wholeness that he already is, and is then revealing that wholeness.

In praying to be free of any problem, Mind can only create challenges and experiences that still reflect the Self. If your Self needs to add to itself some thing or someone, it is still a needing Self. Need equals need. Wholeness equals wholeness. The person who believes in the power of body has his or her attention ever centered on body as a power. Yet, body is but a shadow of consciousness.

The person who is obsessed with losing weight causes Mind to create feelings of self-hate, self-rejection and the person then obsessively and compulsively eats and eats. This person not only eats, but eats those types of food that add pounds.

68

Psalm 24, Verse 1 tells us that "The earth is the Lord's and the fulness thereof"...This means that Principle must be directed by means of our Total Self, that Presence we call God. Some even call it integrity. It means that we are already complete and that as we live and reveal that completeness to the best of our ability our world immediately begins to reflect that completeness at every point. We are here to let God live through us and to permit It to reveal Its integrity in terms of Itself. As we do this, Mind causes every area of our life to conform.

We feel that our desires are good. We take those desires and activate them through our treatments, our prayers. We image, we visualize. We may use will power to bring them into our life. But then they weigh upon us. They are in our experience uneasily. They do not bring happiness. The desire, however, indicates a feeling of incompleteness, of inadequacy.

The images of revealing the Total Self are a different matter. They are not of getting but of giving. It is what we give that we receive.

When we yearn to have the right mate, we are really saying that we ourselves are not the right mate for someone else, that we are not expressing those qualities of love and integrity that we would like to receive from others. Our wanting others to be what we want them to be indicates that we ourselves are not expressing what we desire to experience.

Prayer, for the most part, is the action of trying to get something. Trying to get something takes from us even that which we have. Consciousness always becomes form. Prayer that tries to change others never works because our own "need" is what is directing Mind. That feeling of emptiness is what is going into subconscious Mind and Mind can only create what is fed into It. It is our obsession with shadows—person, place, situation or thing—that touches every area of our life.

True prayer is a letting go of getting. It is a unifying (being at one) with that Power and Presence of life that ALREADY IS. We must individually accept the respon sibility and rise to the level of God. We must use our thought over and over again to touch that inner Center of wholeness. It is that Center that has the answer. It is that Center, when It is expressed, that fills our life with whoever and whatever reflects that Center.

Success in prayer is letting that Power take over and reveal Itself in terms of Itself. It is forever within us. Use your thought to acknowledge It. It has its own purpose. Its own way. To reveal Itself through all that It does as you. It is filled with greatness. Let It have Its way. You will not be sorry.

A woman recently said to me that since we are always our own experience she was feeling terribly guilty about having killed her husband. When I questioned her it was revealed that he had been in an airplane crash and had moved on to the next phase of life. She was misinterpreting what being our own experience means. We only experience our own reaction. Since we are always our own experience and since she had lost her husband, her reasoning was that there must have been something within her consciousness that caused him to be on that plane.

We do not cause other people to die, to lose their jobs or to become ill. That is their consciousness becoming form. We cannot assume a false sense of responsibility about others. We *must assume the responsibility* for *knowing* the *Truth* that *God is all there is.* When we do know this, then we know that they (whoever has passed on, lost their job or whatever) have demonstrated an opportunity to be more completely Self-aware; that their challenge or experience is neither good nor bad.

Our reaction is always our experience. If we are non-attached, non-leaning, then we go on with living life fully and completely. If we are leaning and dependent, we become devastated when someone goes out of our life. We have not assurance or guarantees that the people in our life are going to remain forever.

People often come to me for help because their mate has suddenly left their lives by running off with the secretary, another man or woman, having been in a plane crash or for a great variety of other reasons. Their level of consciousness may have played a part, in that they have grown in one direction and they in another. The direction in which they have gone is their own consciousness becoming form. Our purpose, however, lies not in attaching ourselves to someone else, but in revealing the completeness, the sufficiency, that is within our own Self.

We are not here to add to ourselves. We are here so that God might live through us in terms of Its integrity. This means that we are here to reveal beauty, joy, love and the greatness that God is. We are here to highlight this Presence. We are here to assume the responsibility for our own life, not that of others. We may certainly help another person to discover his or her uniqueness... but the responsibility to reveal that uniqueness lies with the individual.

Most prayer is for the purpose of getting God to do something for us. When we let go of this approach to God and, instead, realize that we are here to reveal God, then that revealing motivation must act upon Mind, causing Mind to produce the forms that represent or reflect that revelation.

Going after a job is a marvelous way to create frustration, resentment, worry and anxiety. Going out to express God, however, frees us of all frustration for we are not trying to get anything. Going on the job

71

interview, and revealing joy, love, enthusiasm and all that God is, can only bring to us the ideal job and opportunity to eternally reveal God. The revealing acts upon Mind and Mind creates the job. Going out as a beggar can only create the job that represents the beggar or that attitude.

When our purpose is to reveal the fullness and magnificence of God, no longer are we trying to protect or defend ourselves. In trying to protect ourselves we are, in effect, saying that there is a power out there that is taking away or preventing our good. Believing in a power out there causes us to have to externally protect ourselves, defend ourselves and to overcome the enemy. This belief is but a shadow of the mind.

It is said that the best defense is a strong offense. To me that means that nothing can work against what we are giving or expressing. If we are expressing God, which is love, then only God can be in our experience. If we are not expecting something from someone, but are instead living to reveal life, our inner integrity, loving to reveal love, pouring out the fullness of our God-Self, then Mind can only create and attract to us that which reflects what we are expressing.

The person who is revealing God does not go around dressed in rags and an unwashed body. We reveal God by looking our best at all times. What we reveal is our treatment or prayer. Mind accepts and creates out of what we reveal. When our purpose is to reveal beauty, joy and love, then we are giving our highest to every moment. When we are revealing God, we are never a burden to anyone. We are self-sufficient and self-reliant.

In looking your best, giving your best, I do not mean that you are forever wearing a tuxedo or gown.

I was given a directive once that said that all ministers should be the perfect example. They should exemplify great prosperity. They should dress beautifully, live in homes of opulence, abundance and order, and they should drive automobiles that radiate wealth and style. This is because we must reveal what we teach. And then the directive went on to say that if the minister has a lower to middle income congregation, he should wear a dark blue suit. If he had an upper income type of congregation, he should wear dark grey. At the human level that may very well be, but at the God-level, we are not here to all look alike or dress alike. It is what we express that counts. What we express must certainly become form. What we think of ourselves is certainly revealed in the way that we dress. However, if we approach life at the level of dress or outer effects, we are working from result rather than cause. Revealing God, which is beauty, manifests as the way that we dress, but God is not the suit or the dress.

Our attention should be centered on knowing Who and What we really are. When our purpose is to reveal God, Its divine qualities, then these qualities become form.

When we love our Self, which is God individualized, this Self-respect does not cause us to rebel or to inflict punishment upon our Self or the world. Revealing God is an exciting purpose because it unifies our Self with our limitless potential. It causes us to acknowledge God as the only power and to identify with the completeness that It already is as our Self.

Chapter 2, Verse 20, of the book of Galatians says, "I live, yet not I, but Christ liveth in me." This is a great principle of revealing the Presence of God. When we acknowledge that Christ is the "I" of our Self, then that "I" lives through all that we think, say and do. This acknowledgment causes us to express in a God-like way, and Mind takes care of everything at the level of form.

When our purpose is to reveal the nature of God in

all that we do, then It is doing all by means of us and nothing can touch us but that which corresponds. We are then the action of giving, of Being. We are not attaching ourselves to anyone else.

It is said that there is a very fine line between love and hate. That is true if we are dealing with the materialistic concept of love. Whenever we are attached to someone, bound to them, depending upon them for our money, courage, strength and love, then we hate when we do not receive what we want. Attachment is not love. Commitment is love. Dependency is not love. Love is being self-responsible. Anger or hate is really a result of depending upon someone and being frustrated because of that dependency. People are never going to be what we want them to be all of the time. They are never going to agree with us or give to us what we desire all of the time. We always resent our being dependent upon someone, yet so many of us do everything we can to build that dependency.

Love seeks nothing of anyone. To put a price on love is saying that we do not know what love is. To say that we love someone and that we have given to him or her of that love in many ways for a certain period of time, and then sue them for a certain amount of money that we believe that love has been worth reveals that we haven't the slightest concept of love. This does not mean to say that in a divorce settlement that we should give up all that we have coming to us by right of consciousness. Love is impartial in that it does not demand anything of anyone. It permits all to be what they are— themselves. At the same time, this is not to be confused with permissiveness. If we love ourselves, we do not permit ourselves to stay in an untenable or uncreative situation.

Every experience is still created out of our Self, of our level of Self-acceptance and Self-love. True love is not based on what we are to get from someone else because the whole purpose of love is to give, to share, to reveal. When we are doing that we attract to ourselves someone who can help us experience mutual love.

We often feel that we have fallen in love with someone. We have found our right and ideal mate, we believe. But we also want them to change their ways so that they will be more acceptable to us and to our friends. This can only mean that we have personalized love, and we are now trying to get rather than to BE. We are now dependent upon that which we want to change. We are now dependent upon someone agreeing with us, doing what we want them to do. Love has departed and dependency has taken over. Mind can then only create the forms and experience of dependency. Dependency takes away our health, freedom, joy, our every good because we only have what we give.

Taking license with this idea and walking out on our families because we want to do our own thing, because we want to be free of others depending upon us, is not love. Love helps others to awaken to their own sufficiency. Love always creates a mutual experience, not a selfish one. Love is a "we" experience, not a me action.

Self-sufficiency is the only possible way to know the true meaning of love. When we are self-sufficient we automatically help others to be likewise. So many people have been trained by their parents and friends to look to someone else for their good. They are taught to look for a mate who will take care of them, provide for them, who will give to them their every good. And so they have gotten married, not as an expression of love, but as a way of being secure. They soon discover that no person can bring us happiness. Happiness is the action of giving our integrity to all that we do. Happiness is the action of giving. Yes, what we send out must come back so we receive as well. But that is automatic and the

75

true happiness is in the giving while we appreciate that which comes back to us.

So much of the liberation movement is seen to be a way of destroying families, but it is not. Each person must be liberated into thinking for himself and coming up with what he or she is really all about.

We must all realize that we are not here to be the slaves of anyone. Slavery is dependency and is always a choice we make for ourselves. We can only be enslaved when we have looked for our good outside of our own Self, rather than from within our own Being. Each person has to arrive at that point where he is assuming the responsibility for his own life, for his own good. When he does this he also helps others do the same for themselves. We only develop ulcers because of our dependency. We are free of them through our independency.

I have often been told by others that since they love me, they have a right to tell me about all of the things that I am doing wrong. They feel that it is only for my own good that I change my ways. They feel that their criticism is constructive and therefore necessary. Is their so-called love not one of dependency? They want me to conform to them so that they will feel comfortable, so that I now depend upon them, so that my dependency upon them will show that they are right and I am wrong. Is this love? No.

They certainly have a right to reveal how they feel. We have a responsibility to evaluate for ourselves. When we dare to assume our own responsibility for our lives and know that we stand at the center of it, then we know that all change in our experience is self-change and we begin to do something about changing the outer through changing the inner.

If we read any of the letters to persons who give advice to the lovelorn, we see dependency in action. They may either be asking advice, criticizing, or talking about certain people in their lives who are not behaving the way that they should. Love always acknowledges my own self-worth and the wholeness of others. My self-acceptance says that there is that within me that knows what to do, what to give, what to share.

Love that I am knowing for my Self first of all frees me of that false sense of responsibility of being in charge of the lives of others. Love that I am knowing for my Self causes me to do my own work, my own thinking and to go through my own challenges. It does not permit me to be a burden to anyone.

Resentment is a result of dependency. Hatred is a result of looking to others for our good. Fear is the result of dependency. So is jealousy. Every destructive emotion is a result of depending upon other than our own Self. We must let go of looking for anything from anyone and assume the responsibility for directing Mind with the idea, feeling and action of sufficiency. Mind then takes care of the details.

We all know people who complain eternally about others. They talk about them, downgrade them, criticize them and become angry about them. They are doing this because of their dependency upon them. They are doing this because they are not living out of their own sufficiency. They are not Self-aware. Self-awareness is love. It acknowledges the Presence and Power within our own Being. It acknowledges the same within all who are in our lives.

In not minding our own business, we have the hate or the personal love that can be loving one moment and turn to hate the next if the object of the love does not agree or come through. God is love, and this love is independent of anyone as being cause. This love is impersonal, in that it is non-leaning, non-attached. God is love and God is impartial. God is not a taker. It is a giver.

God does not judge. It lives. It IS. The love that we are revealing, being impartial, directs Mind, through sufficiency, and thus every relationship is creative. It is creative because it demands that we respect ourselves as well as others.

All of this Principle that we are discussing is of no use to anyone if it is not practiced. Treatment is no good unless it brings one to the point where one is free of the anxiety. It is no good unless it brings one to that point where the feeling of wholeness is realized. It does no good unless one arrives at that feeling where God, which is love, takes over and lives through us. This is our purpose, our goal. Nobody arrives at the destination without practice, practice, practice. If we are not doing it now, it is not a part of our life.

When I was a child I was given piano lessons. Since they were thought, by my parents, to be very expensive, I was told that all of this money should not go to waste and that I had to practice every day. I finally arrived at that point where I was a fairly accomplished pianist. If I had practiced more than that, I would have been even more accomplished. I gave them up when I went into the army and then to school after that.

Years later, I rented an apartment in New York City that had a piano in it. I sat down at it one day and tried to play all of the songs that I had memorized years before. I discovered that I had forgotten them. More than that, my fingers no longer seemed to work. I could no longer play the piano. I had to start all over again.

What we do not practice fades away from our consciousness. Treatment is the same. Living the Presence is the same. It must be practiced over and over again. This is our own individual responsibility. No one can do it for us.

With practice we arrive at that point where merely

acknowledging the Presence brings us to that point where It takes over.

The way we do anything is also a statement going into Mind. It is a treatment. If we give our integrity to all that we do, we can only reap the great rewards that this produces. Whatever we are doing is an opportunity to live the Presence. The way we write, speak, walk, act and express. Mind always creates the forms of what we are thinking, doing and the way that we are doing it.

I have a large and flowing handwriting. I try to maintain the standards of legibility and spontaneity that it represents. Many of my students who have gotten handwritten letters from me felt that they could become more like me by changing their handwriting to be more like mine. Those who used to write with very small and precise lettering began writing boldly and sweepingly. Many began writing just like I do. There are handwriting experts who can tell your personality by your handwriting. It reflects your consciousness. I am not saying that if you write boldly and in a large, sweeping style that your personality will change, however.

Don't try to imitate someone else because then your own uniqueness will be forsaken. But when you write, know that it is God writing by means of you. Know that there is an intelligence guiding and directing your way. Know that the greatness of God as you is being expressed in terms of Itself. Practice knowing this and revealing it when you not only write but when you do everything.

Self-authority just doesn't happen. We have to earn it by revealing it ALWAYS. Each and every moment is a golden opportunity to live and reveal Self-authority. Be your God-Self in action. Any person who is accomplished in what they are doing has consciously practiced, over and over again, their special talents. They have awakened to the genius of their Self and they have dared to express that genius in what they do.

Energy is not something that we get. It is something that we reveal. It is already there. Practice revealing energy, enthusiasm, joy and love in all that is done and they are ours. With this deliberate practice of the Presence, we arrive at a point where it is automatic, where it is ingrained in our personality. Even though we are already complete, it takes practice in believing it. It takes practice in getting it out into expression. There is no power in our life except that which we are expressing. We only have what we express.

If we believe in something apart from or unlike our Ideal Self, we begin to express that belief. When we choose to experience love, we must first of all express love.

We must not worry about tomorrow. It is what we are practicing and revealing in the present moment that is directing Mind. It is what we are doing and the way we are doing it right now that counts. Even though our prayers, treatments and expression of yesterday is still in subconscious Mind, all is being controlled by what we are doing right now. Mind is always causing body to correspond to this now expression. When we are at one with the Ideal, our fears are automatically gone. When we are the action of revealing our Ideal-Self, nothing can touch us but that which corresponds to this ideal.

We must identify with wholeness, completeness, with the Ideal. Identify with the qualities of God and actively practice expressing them. We can practice the Presence in every step that we take, in every word that we speak, in every single thing that we do. In order to learn to do it, we have to do it. We must begin where we are, right now.

We must assume the responsibility for living our own

life. We are unique, each of us is very special. That uniqueness is not an excuse to live in a mediocre or demeaning way.

You may say that your job or present situation is not created out of greatness. That does not make any difference to God. No matter what the situation, we can fill the present moment with the qualities of God. No matter where we are we can actively know that God is everywhere present and that It is present by means of each one of us right where we are. We can fill this moment with all that we believe God to be. God is not a person but action. We can fill this moment with love, joy, abundance, health, prosperity, excitement and enthusiasm. Nobody can do this for us.

Our day is created out of our own Self. Our Self is always in action, in one way or another. We must KNOW Who and What we truly are, and then practice revealing all of these God-like qualities that are ours to reveal and to share. Practice. Practice. Practice. We only have what we are expressing right now.

If we are to live fully, then the time has come for us to assume the responsiblity of thinking and living out of our own Self. The time has come to stop thinking in terms of trying to be healthy and wealthy and having the right mate. All of these indicate a lack of Self-awareness. The answer to all challenges lies in knowing Who and What we really are and then moving out into the world to express this greatness that we have to give to all who are on our pathway.

People want healings and they get them, only to come back again for another. I counseled with one woman whose entire time was taken up with the pursuit of health and a man. She belonged to several of those organizations that find you the right mate. The men that were provided were always lacking in something. They had certain faults that were unforgivable. Each time that she came for treatment it was to get a healing or a different man. We had to toss aside that approach and work with assuming self-responsibility and the expressing of those qualities that provide health and draw to us desirable people. She made both of her demonstrations when she stopped chasing her good and began living it.

If forever looking outside of our Self for our good, we always have physical problems. There is more to life than health or the right mate. There is more to life than any thing that we could possibly name. Since every experience is created out of our Self, then we must use our thought to awaken that Total Self within us that is already complete. We must think in ways of giving rather than getting. This is completely contrary to the human way, which always desires something, but the law is still the law. WE ONLY HAVE WHAT WE GIVE.

Living out of our own Self-authority is infinitely more important than anything or anyone. What good is having that ideal home if we are not free to be our own Self in it? What good is having our ideal mate if we are not free of their dominance and control? If someone tells you that if you really loved him or her, you would behave in a different way, and if you give in for that reason, you have lost your Self-authority. That is not love. If someone threatens you to take away something that you hold dear and you react with fear, then you have failed to realize that no one can take away your good, and that nothing is worth having if it takes away our self-respect, our Self-authority.

The beggar in life is looking for good from someone else. If we are always concerned with what other people are thinking about us, then we are a beggar. If we are forever afraid of hurting others, then they are calling the shots rather than we ourselves. If this is our pattern, we are directing Mind all the while as a beggar rather than directing Mind with the authority of expressing what we are really all about. We must dare to be our God-Self in action, and when we do this we will not permit ourselves to be intimidated by the personalities and hang-ups of others.

There is more to life than health. There is living with Self-authority. Without that there is no health. Health does not come first and then Self-authority. It is the other way around.

Let us use our thought to identify with that Self that we truly are. Let us let go of appearances and deal with this cause to our experience. Self. Which is God individualized. In this awareness of Who and What we really are there are no motivations of trying to put something over on someone. We don't need to. It is only ego, a sense of inadequacy, that needs to do that. Be true to our God-Self. Be true to our Self-integrity.

When others behave in ways that do not represent our Self-integrity, we must not judge them. But we do not need to have in our experience that which does not represent our Self. If we judge it or fight it, then we are making sure that it remains in our experience. People only want to judge us because they are unsure of their own Self. If we want to change others, this reveals the same thing about ourselves.

Since the law of our Self is forever in action, then we must let go of trying to do something about the world and we must use our time, our energies and intelligence to identify with thoughts and ideas of greatness about our Self. We must explore this uniqueness that we are. We must be at one with this True Self that knows no disease, lack or limitation. We must dare to be this Self in action. Mind creates the opportunities for us to prove our Self-authority and Self-integrity.

If we are actively daring to express our God-Self, then

the challenges that come to us are met and gone through in terms of our integrity.

Power is not something that we have over others or that others have over us. Power is knowing the Truth of our Being and letting Mind take care of the details. Power is the acknowledgment that we are already complete. Power is the letting go of trying to do something about someone else and, instead, living out of our own inner authority. Self-authority is greater than health because it produces health. In always looking for our good from the right man or the right woman, we have to give up whatever they do not like. We must function for their approval. We are then being led like a dog on a leash and are commanded to sit, stand, beg, whine or speak on command.

We are not here to live like that. We are here to reveal the Presence of God. We are here to live out of our own self-sufficiency and to share our Self with others. The moment we do anything in order to get something, we have given up our Self-authority. The moment we let someone talk us into feeling guilty about our living out of our Self-integrity, then we are trying to get rather than to BE.

There is more to life than what we can get from someone else. Just to have someone in our life so that we won't be lonely will not free us from being lonely. Having a long list of things that we want to demonstrate does not bring security, or even those things. That list simply indicates a great sense of emptiness within our Self.

Let us consciously identify with that Presence, that completeness. Let us make this our reason for being. Let us express and reveal this God-Self in any and every situation. The expression then becomes our demonstration. We automatically have what we express. Mind can only create that which represents and reflects our Self-expression. Life is our expression, not the results. Life

is the action of giving out rather than the anxiety about
bringing in.

If that good that you desire seems to be bringing with
it frustration, fear, anger, anxiety, then whatever it is is
not worth it. The thing is symptomatic of an identity that
needs, rather than gives. This can all be changed by
using thought to identify with Spirit. God contemplating
Itself in terms of Itself by means of each of us.

Most of us desire and want success. We do a great deal
to make sure that we attain that success. This is
necessary. However, when we are doing something and
doing it only because it will bring us what we desire,
then we are not doing what we are doing with joy or
enthusiasm. We have made the thing, the goal, our point
of attention and we are by-passing the real meaning and
experience of success. Most of success is directed to what
we are going to get. We often define success in terms
of the things that we have already gotten. But it is what
we are *doing in the now* that counts. It is *what we are doing
now and the way we are doing it* that is directing Mind.

Success is not some thing. Success is an action, it is
an expression, that is now taking place. It is giving of
the highest of our Self to whatever we are now doing
for the sheer joy of doing, of working, of giving. When
there is thought of a reward, we are trying to get, and
we automatically are controlled by a belief in a power
outside of Self. In trying to get, we are always going to
know anxiety, fear, perhaps anger, but always frustration when what we want is not forthcoming, or does
not come quickly enough.

It is true that Mind always produces results, that consciousness always becomes form, and that what we give
comes back to us in kind. This is just the law of our Being
in action. We can never get away from the law of our
Self. When we are manipulating others in order to
get something, the joy and the enthusiasm of simply

expressing our God-Self is not there. Something else creeps in. The motivation of getting always limits the expression of Self, the giving. One who goes forth as a beggar is never free. One who is afraid that something will be taken away from him is never free. If we are working desperately only so that we can hang on to our jobs, that desperation will always be with us and it will diminish the quality and the joy of our work.

Work is God in action. It is meant to be a divine opportunity to reveal the potential, the greatness and the wholeness that is already within our Self. This cannot be revealed if we are trying to get.

If success means to us living in a mansion in the best part of town, then we are going to have to do whatever we have to do in order to get and maintain that home. When something or someone owns us, we are not free. When we are not free, we demonstrate aches and pains. When we are not free to be our own person it could manifest as asthma. When we realize that our reason for being, however, is to work, to reveal the nature of our God-Self in all that we do, then there is freedom. Work is the purpose, the goal, the reality. Because the law of our Self is always in action, then what we do and the way we do it determines the things that come into our lives.

When we work in order to express our Self fully and fearlessly, the quality of our work is greater than it is when we are working under tension. Tension is only there because of fear. Fear is there because we are living for what we are going to get rather than for the sheer joy of expressing our God-Self. By the same token, talking about what we have already done takes us away from doing something creative right now.

Those who live in the past are not really living. We are only living when we are doing something joyfully and creatively in the present moment.

Jealousy is the result of trying to get. Love, on the other hand, is that which gives and is not concerned with the reward. Jealousy, therefore, has nothing to do with love. It represents insecurity and insecurity always tries to get.

Success, just as love, cannot be measured. It is not to be found in any amount of money or even as that mansion. There is nothing wrong with money or the luxurious home. But they should be the natural results of our having expressed ourselves uniquely and fearlessly. Success is not worthwhile if we are controlled by the things in our life.

No thing is really worthwhile if there are strings attached, if it brings with it anxiety. No thing can bring freedom because freedom is non-attachment. Freedom is living, it is BEING, it is working for the sake of revealing the qualities of our Ideal Self.

Success to many is outdoing someone else. It has a competitive undercurrent, and thus competition never permits pure joy to be expressed. It may act as a catalyst, but one is controlled by what one is competing against. Trying to win over others is looking for results. When we believe in and love ourselves we give our highest to all that we do and we are not devastated if someone else comes in first. When we must win at all costs our work becomes inferior rather than free, inspired and divinely guided. In working for the applause of the world, one has to give the world what it wants. Since we cannot satisfy everyone, we are torn if this is what we are trying to do. When seeking to please everyone, we are not free. We are not free when we try to please even just one person. However, in working for the sake of discovering new facets within our Self, for the sake of revealing the Presence of God, then unfoldment is that which takes place. With unfoldment comes the effects automatically, but our true reward is really the work, the Self-expression.

Too many of us pray and work in order to get. We fail to realize that our real demonstration is the revealing of our Ideal Self. Work is its own reward. Each of us is created so that God might reveal Itself in terms of Itself through us. God does not seek rewards. It does not seek to attain success. It is already complete. God as each of us is the action of giving, FOR THE SAKE OF GIVING, FOR THE SAKE OF REVEALING THE NATURE OF GOD. This is what success is really all about. We must trust Mind to take care of the results. It has always done exactly that. If we seem to have gotten the short end of the stick, it is only because we were looking for a reward. No matter what we do, we always get back what we give.

Our Self-expression is the real power in our lives. It is the reality of our Self. And it is its own reward. This is our true demonstration. A great actress is only a great actress as long as she is acting and as long as she is expressing greatness. And so it is with any profession. Many people go into certain professions because of the rewards. Because of the money and the applause. Many of these people have nervous breakdowns. They become tense and fearful. It is only because they are after the rewards rather than the Self-expression.

It seems to be the goal of so many to get as much as possible for as little as possible. The failure's dream is to get something for nothing. But we only receive what we are giving and the way that we are giving it.

Let us let go of the rewards. They are always there. Let us let go of the results and concentrate on revealing enthusiasm, love, joy, integrity, health, wealth, and success. We can pour all of these qualities into all that we do. Since our point of attention is always our experience, then it behooves us to keep our attention on that which will permit us to live in freedom and greatness.

When we are trying to get even with someone, we are

activating a negative idea in our own consciousness and so our problem remains. There is a much better way to go through our challenges than to criticize, condemn or to undermine the person we feel is responsible. Whoever seems to be doing something to us is only there helping us fulfill the law of our own Being.

There is power in neglect. What we do not give our attention to fades away. Nothing can remain in our experience if there is nothing to maintain it. Mind is attaining and maintaining ONLY that which represents our now use of thought. To deny the problem, to worry about it, to even pray about it, is still giving it our attention, and so it remains. Be involved with the Truth and the Truth sets us free.

Since we are dealing with Principle, the law of mind, then we can use it to be free of anything that does not represent our True Self, as long as we keep our attention on our True Self. This also brings into our experience whoever and whatever does represent this Self that we are expressing. Many married men and women come to me for consultation, and they start out by complaining about their mates. They blame the other person for what is going wrong. Yet we are always our own experience.

Every marriage has to be earned every day. Each has to be supported, sustained and maintained. This has to be done each and every day or it begins to fade away. Just being legally wed does not create a marriage. It is an ongoing challenge that must be faced in a loving and creative way. If there is neglect, then what we neglect goes out of our life. The principle is still the same for every situation. We can create any experience we choose out of the moment, out of our own Self. But we only have what we ourselves are now giving.

If we are always busy reacting to the distractions of the world, we will never hear the voice of our own divine purpose within our Self. We must neglect the voices of the world and begin to listen to the voice within our own Self. When we acknowledge that voice, then we hear it strong and clear.

We only have what we give. This idea cannot be repeated enough. It is something that we have to learn over and over again. In order to be in charge of our own lives, we must be giving our Self to others every moment. We must dare to be and express ourselves. We are not here to be entertained by an eternal television or the voices of the world. When we are filling this present moment with the authority and the power of our God-Self, then Mind can create the forms of our expression. We have to earn our good each and every day and it is what we ourselves are giving that tells Mind what to do. We must not look to others. We must assume the responsibility and live out of our own Self-authority.

A survey was made of an experiment that included teachers, school children and their parents and it revealed some very interesting results. It had become the way of life for children to watch about four or five hours of television each day. School teachers were becoming alarmed at the growing trend of their students' behavior. With the cooperation of the parents, television viewing was limited to one hour a day for each child. After a few withdrawal pains the children showed in their classes and in their play periods more originality, more uniqueness, more creativity. They began to function with more self-sufficiency. They began to give more. The survey concluded that television is not a particularly good thing if it is not kept in its place because it keeps us from going within to our own inner kingdom.

Anything that takes us away from living out of our own Self gets in the way of living. When we fail to look within, Mind creates only the results of not living vitally, enthusiastically or excitingly. Life is an individual experience and we cannot entrust our good, our lives, to someone else. We must assume the individual responsibility of breathing life into our work, our relationships, our purpose.

No one "out there" has any power over our lives unless we give it to them. If we are not "standing up and being counted," then we are sitting down and being counted out. Being intimidated by someone else simply says that we are not daring to be our Self. We must let go of what they are doing and put our full attention upon what we are doing right now.

Too much of our attention is put upon what someone else is doing instead of our own Self-action. We must release others to their own experience of Self, whatever that may be, and center our attention on Who and What we are. Yes, we can help others awaken to their uniqueness, we can give them strokes, but we cannot live their lives for them.

A child learns to swear because they are imitating us or because of our shocked reaction to their swearing. When we do not react, they see that they are not pushing our buttons. Someone calls on the telephone and begins to make obscene suggestions. If we are shocked, talk back and react greatly, we can expect another phone call. We must simply hang up and get busy with living out of our own Self-authority. There is power in neglect and there is power in attention, in giving. Give what you choose to experience and release that which you do not.

KNOWING THAT GOD IS THE REALITY AND NATURE OF MY SELF, AND KNOWING THAT GOD IS ALWAYS AN INDIVIDUAL EXPERIENCE, I ASSUME THE RESPONSIBILITY OF ETERNALLY BEING AT ONE WITH THIS PRESENCE OF COMPLETENESS. I RELEASE THE PEOPLE IN MY WORLD AS BEING CAUSE TO MY EXPERIENCE IN ANY WAY WHATSOEVER. I BEGIN RIGHT NOW TO LIVE, TO

REVEAL, THE PRESENCE OF GOD. I AM THE AUTHORITY IN MY LIFE. I AM THE POWER IN MY EXPERIENCE. KNOWING THAT THE I THAT I AM AS GOD PERMITS ME TO GIVE IN JOYFUL AND GLORIOUS WAYS. MY EVERY EXPERIENCE IS CREATED OUT OF MY ACTIVE SELF-KNOWING-NESS. I POUR INTO EXPRESSION THE JOY, LOVE, ENTHUSIASM AND VITALITY OF GOD FOR I KNOW THAT IT IS ALWAYS GOD REVEALING ITSELF BY MEANS OF ME. I ASSUME THE RESPONSIBILITY, THIS I THAT GOD IS AS ME. I AM FREE NOW AND ALWAYS TO ACT, TO GIVE AND TO SHARE, AND MIND CREATES ALL THAT REPRESENTS THIS I THAT I AM IN NEW AND WONDERFUL WAYS.

CHAPTER IV

Go
Further

Until we arrive at the realization of Who and What we really are we can go no further than where we are right now. Our lives are made up of the things and the people who represent our level of Self awareness, our level of Self-love. Our tomorrows become a repetition of our yesterdays until we choose to look at our Self in a new and greater way today. There is that within each of us that desires to go further, that seeks to experience itself in new and greater ways. Since we are Life's means to experience Itself, we are here to move forward. We are not meant to stand still.

So often people are going nowhere in life and they are filled with frustration, anger and fear. They say, "There is no excitement in my life. Life is dull, dull, dull. I have no friends, no opportunities. There is no reason for living." To say this is to believe that we have no power over our destinies. We are dealing with a shadow of the Mind. We are trying to get rather than to let an inner Power fill our consciousness and live through all that we do. Life is naturally boring if one day is the same as the previous one. Life is unexciting if we do not venture out with Self-authority to experiment, to take chances, to do something different. Life is boring if we do not dare to make a mistake.

When I first discovered the Science of Mind I became aware of the Law of Mind that would help me make sure that everything happened the way that I wanted it to happen. I used to protect myself from making any mistakes. That was my first mistake. Stagnation soon set in and life was not as exhilarating as it should have been. When we have a program that does not vary we are eliminating spontaneity from our experience. I realized that in directing Mind so completely I was outlining everything. I was trying to tell God what to do. I had thus taken myself out of the experience of God.

When we are Self-aware, when we know Who and What we truly are, we dare to express ourselves in new and experimental ways. We dare to be innovative. The world may call it failure, but if we are letting our inner voice guide and direct us into new endeavors, new ways, then it cannot be failure. It is simply Self-expression. When we love our Self we do not know what failure is. When we accept our Self we dare to experiment. Experimenting is letting go of that which was and permitting something new to come forth.

The more we refer to and trust this inner Self, the more innovative we become. In looking for ways to make sure that our good happens, we are locking ourselves into sameness. Without this realized inner Self we live at the level of conformity. We thus receive the things of the world rather than of our divine potential. When we give attention to this inner Self, new and greater ideas come through and we begin to dare to listen to them and to put them into action. Then, Life is no longer an effort but a living of the Presence, an expression of our highest Self. At this level one does not strive for one's good. One realizes that it already IS.

If we measure our Self by the forms in our life, we are still tying ourselves to things. Too many people believe that the more money and the more things they have the more secure they are. Money and things do not bring security. They can disappear in the twinkling of an eye. To try to measure our consciousness by whether we are driving a "status car" is to say that the power in our lives is in the automobile.

If we look into our wallet or purse right now and find $500,000, we may say that we are wealthy. We are then looking to our wallet to tell us what the situation is. The following day we may look in the same place and find only $1.00. We then must say that we are poor. This is dealing with shadows rather than reality.

If we try to do all of the things that others are doing because it has brought them worldly success, we can very easily fail. Why? What works for some does not necessarily work for another. We must let go of imitating others. We must learn to listen to the within. Listen to the voice of our own uniqueness and let it take us beyond where we are in life right now. We can go further by letting go of person, place and thing as being the authority in our own life.

There are all kinds of classes on teaching you to do things the way that someone else has done them before. This is all very well and good, but there can be a danger of every group trying to be just like everyone else. There is a danger of services to the public becoming repetitious, based upon what someone else has already done.

> We can only go further by delving into the uniqueness of our own Self. We can only go further by letting go of what someone else is doing and discovering our own way.

We can only go further by not attaching ourselves to our demonstrations, the good that we are seeking. Life is a grand adventure. We must learn to let go of that which was and to let something new come in. It happens when we are willing to acknowledge this inner Presence and to let It take over and guide with Its Infinite Intelligence. This is the voice of our own True Self.

We can pray and pray for things. We can demonstrate them. Yet if we desire to truly go further in life, we must let go of everything and everyone.

We must let the law of our Being attract, attain and maintain. We must let go of the goals that are based upon getting and begin to live. Begin to live by using our thought to arrive at the realization of What and Who we really are. Identify with authentic Center of our Being.

Whenever we have conflict in our consciousness, is it not because we are trying to get something? Is it not because we are trying to make something happen? Is it not because we are attached to proven ways of doing things? Yet each day is different. Times are changing and we must come up with our own answers for living in the now. We must not be afraid to experiment, to take a chance.

Our good resides in "letting go and letting God." This means that we trust this inner voice that is self-reliant and is seeking to go further than where we are right now. Our good is to be found in releasing everyone in our life as being our power and realizing that we are the power. We are not our body, nor the people in our world, nor the money in our bank account. I am that I am. Body, money, things, and people are results. They are the forms of our consciousness.

To live the Presence of God is to have the forms, but now they are all the forms of God. They are now forms that reflect God's completeness and perfection. God is the action of never repeating Itself. We go further by daring to let new ideas, new purpose, come in. We must dare to experiment. We must dare to make a mistake. We must dare to do something new.

The "human" approach to life rose to the fore to a great degree during the time of diminished gasoline allocations to Southern California. Many people tried to get their own gas tanks filled at the expense of others. There were those who schemed to obtain gasoline even though it meant that others had to go without. Those of us who were in the gas lines for hours saw others try to pull in ahead of us. Sometimes they got away with it. Other times those who had been in line for all of those hours would scream and carry on to such an extent that the line crashers would storm away chagrined and angry. The "human" way is to protect oneself at all costs, to make sure that one gets one's own good no matter what. Yet this approach is again dealing with shadows of the mind. It is living at the level of belief that our good comes from outside of our Self.

When one is even using the Science of Mind to protect oneself, it is saying that there is a power out there— that someone or something can take away or withhold our good. All the while the law of our Being is in action. However we are directing Mind...that we must experience.

If we believe that our good is out there, then we have to resort to intimidation in order to protect ourselves. We have to outwit others to make sure that we get ours and they don't get theirs.

Every time we treat or use Mind in order to "get" we are, in fact, denying that our good already is. Every time we try to add to our Self we are telling Mind that we are not already complete, that we lack in many or all ways. At the "human" level we expect something from others. We expect or want to be taken care of by them. We demand what we believe is rightfully or not-so-rightfully ours. The mere demanding directs Mind to take away even that which we have. It is still and always will be the law of life that we only receive what we first of all give.

We only have what we are expressing. Self-preservation is a denial of God, of the Total Self. Trying to defend our Self says that we believe that there is something to defend our Self from. There is nothing outside of our Self. All there is is Self. Being Self-aware is our greatest protection. Being Self-aware is our true defense. We can only experience our Self. It may be true that we have to "take our turn in line." It is also true that all of this time can be utilized in creative ways. It need not be wasted time. Each and every challenge is an opportunity to be Self-aware, to make a demand upon our own inner God-Self.

We are only happy when we are doing our own work, living out of our own sufficiency, and we cannot experience this if we try to get others to "fill our tanks" for us. We must fill our own. In trying to protect ourselves we have to rely on more and more weapons, more and more physical power. But this has never been the answer. No war has ever solved anything. Having to fight to protect one's Self is a result of having looked at our Self incorrectly. True power is in GIVING, in BEING, in LIVING, not in getting.

Look at most public figures. Is it not a good example of self-preservation? Each one attacks the other, blames the other, criticizes the other. This only reveals that there is insecurity about what they themselves are doing. Whenever we blame someone else we are revealing that we ourselves have not been producing anything worthwhile.

Whenever we are worried about what is going to happen, we are revealing that we are not giving our best to the present moment. In having to organize to protect reputation, salary, job, relationships, we are directing Mind to create anxiety, fear, the opportunities to fight, lie, cheat, defend, all at someone else's expense. All of these are but shades of the Mind because we can only see or hear that which is within our own consciousness.

Everything in our experience is created out of the Self, and no one else is cause to our experience. Mind can only create for us all that represents our Self—nothing more and nothing less. The need to be protected creates the necessity of being protected. To know that we are God's means to be releases us from that need, for nothing can touch us but that which reflects our Self.

If the world is to know peace and love, then it still must be individually experienced and expressed. The world cannot save us. We are always our very own experience. To identify with the idea that we are already whole and complete is to know that we do not need to be protected. To know that we are already full is to permit our individualization of that wholeness to go forth to direct Mind in ways of wholeness. Wholeness realized must become visible. If wholeness is individually realized, then Mind cannot produce experiences of limitation. Mind can only create experiences of peace, love, and abundance.

When we are secure in knowing Who and What we really are, there is no need to take advantage of others. Why? It is our now purpose to give rather than to take. Since we are created in the image and likeness of God, then we are and always shall BE. We no longer have to preserve our good at the expense of others for our good automatically IS. It is within the Self. The Self comes automatically equipped with all good.

We are not living in a world of cruelty or harshness unless we believe in these shadows of the mind. If we see the world as being an ugly and cruel place, we are imposing something upon the world. Our own consciousness. The world is always a reaction to our own action. The world can only respond to what we are knowing, feeling and expressing, for that is the way that Mind works.

In not having to defend our Self, this does not mean that we lay down and let others walk all over us. It does not mean that we retire to a quiet corner and shut up. No indeed. In living the Presence of God we very actively express our Self-belief, our Self-esteem. We announce to the world Who and What we are by daring to live out of our Self-integrity. Otherwise the world does not know how to respond. If one wants to put it this way, one could say that "self-preservation is Self-expression."

Acknowledge the Godness of your Self and simply let this Presence live through all that you say, think, and do. Go forth as the action and expression of joy and love...and that is what you receive. The law of your Self cannot be infringed upon in any way.

We are not handcuffed to certain people. They are there because of our consciousness, for no other reason. Change the way we think about our Self and we change our experience with those people. Dare to be our Self in action and they react accordingly.

We are always giving to every moment. What we are giving to others we are really giving to ourselves. What we express at any time always comes back to us. Since there is really but one Self in our experience, then we are not only the Self of our children, our mate...we are the Self of our friends, of our pets, of our neighbors, etc. What does this mean? When we seem to be giving to someone else, we are essentially giving to our Self for we always receive what we give. What we send out comes back to us in kind. It may seem to come to us from someone else but it is really coming through them like a boomerang that we have sent out. It is as if we are taking money out of our right pocket and transferring it to the left. It is as though we are making a deposit in our own bank account. We give out and it comes back.

In our growing experience of prosperity we must not believe that we are giving out of a limited supply and that what we give depletes that supply. We are not really taking money out of our wallet, but out of the Source that is forever full. What we give never really leaves us for consciousness always becomes form. We can go further, then, in our larger degree of living by acknowledging that Source that we are individualizing, that is forever complete, no matter what the direction is of our giving. We are really giving from and to the greater concept of that Self. Mind can only bring back in kind what we are truly giving.

By the same token, if we give to the idea of someone else's insufficiency, then we are giving to our own insufficiency, and that is what we must experience. In feeling sorry for others, we are seeing their lack. That lack is really our own shadow of the mind. Others are interpretations of our own Self.

We are bombarded with books and magazine articles about what to do about the great troubles that are coming our way. We are told that if we are smart we will do certain things to take advantage of a negative situation. We are told that we have got to be prepared with worldly goods if we are to outsmart a financial crash that is certain to come. Prosperity, however, is consciousness, not things. Things are there as a result of consciousness. If ours is the consciousness of fear, of poverty, we will seek to add to ourselves one thing after another...we will endeavor to be prepared for this catastrophe that is heading our way. When the catastrophe is something within our own consciousness it becomes form, in one way or another. Instead of preparing ourselves for the "coming bad times" at the level of hoarding, we must build the consciousness of Truth. We are only prepared for any challenge by knowing Who and What we really are. By believing in our Self. We can only go further in life by going further with a greater concept of our Self.

Acknowledge that True Self that can do anything. Acknowledge that Self within that knows what to do. Identify with It and express It. Give of It to It. If one sees one's Self as being poor, one will give of poorness to poorness...one will give in a very small and constricted way and thus will receive in a very small way. That's the way Mind works. It can only create out of the beliefs given to It. If one gives in order to get, one is not really giving. Rather, one is looking for a return. That means that one is looking for a return outside of one's Self. But there is nothing outside of our Self. It is all within.

We are told to forgive our enemies. This is exact principle! Those who have offended really represent our own self-judgment. The forgiveness of anyone is really the forgiving of our own Self, for there is only ONE Self in our experience. We are always dealing with our own Self. When our Self is acknowledged to be "I", and "I" being God, then we have set aside all judgment and we are always dealing with our True Self.

Hating someone else is really hating our own Self because there is nothing outside of our Self. Judging someone else is only a result of not being aware of Who and What we really are. When we love and appreciate ourselves we do not judge. When we have a high level of self-esteem we do not judge. Love does not judge. It sees wholeness, beauty and love regardless of where it is looking. Because of what we are expressing, Mind can only call to our attention that which represents our Self-expression. That is why the answer to every challenge is to let go of doing something about someone else and do something about our own use of thought.

Giving is the action of recognizing that there is but one Source and that It is forever complete. When we truly give we are giving of that Source to that Source, this eternal fullness, and thus we demonstrate fullness in every area of our life. we go further by looking beyond the shadows and dealing only with Truth—the Truth that there is but one power. Identify with this Total Self and that is what we must express. That is what we must give. We are always giving to the law of our own being, to the law of our own Self. Mind makes visible our identity, whatever that may be.

There is a gold mine within our Self. It is not "out there," although it may manifest "out there." Invest in this gold mine of our own Self. The concept of "God as me" is forever full, it is always complete.

Prosperity is not money, although it results in money. Love is not a significant other, although it may result in significant others. Success is not applause, applause may be there. Prosperity, love and success are always what we express. They are expressions of a high level of self-esteem. When we try to get money, we are saying that money is the power, the reality. But money has no power. It cannot think. It cannot act. It cannot do.

Our significant others are only in our lives because of what we are giving and expressing. The law of our Self has attracted them to us. When we say, "I love you," to what appears to be someone else, that person really represents our own consciousness. He or she represents the visibleness of our Self, of our Self-expression. So we are really expressing love from our Self to our Self. We have what we give. Mind always brings back what we send out. The people and things in our life are but shadows of the mind. Love is a great power because it makes no judgment. It is magnificent power because it gives unreservedly of itself and asks nothing in return.

Prosperity is love. It is demonstrating greater ways to give of its nature. When we go within our own Self and make a demand upon that Self, we discover new and greater talents that are ours to use, share and to express.

103

Expressing prosperity, love, for the sake of expressing prosperity and love must manifest as money or whatever form the expression takes. It all goes out from the Self and returns to the Self as whatever is required to prove that Self.

In order to be free to go further, to live in a greater way, we must be free of the influence of others. If we have ever been maltreated, controlled, or walked over by others, it is not because they were going against our wishes or taking advantage of us. They were doing what they were doing because, in some way, we taught them to do exactly that. If we do not dare to speak up for our Self, then we are making a statement anyway and we are telling them that they are giving us exactly what we want. No one knows what we are really all about unless we reveal what is going on within us. If we say nothing, this is an invitation for them to take charge.

To realize that others are only to us what we permit them to be, that they are what we are to ourselves, is to stop blaming them. We cease begging and beseeching and make our demands upon our own Self. All we have to work with is our Self. Our every experience is created out of this Self. If we permit someone to move in ahead of us in any kind of a line, we are teaching not only them, but the law of Mind, that we do not count. We are thus teaching Mind to bring into our experience others who will move in and push us aside. We are never dealing with someone else. We are always dealing with our own Self. All of the people in our lives are really shadows of the Mind.

We must actively acknowledge Who and What we really are—an individualization of God—then we can begin to express this Self-authority. Without this expression Mind can only create whatever it is that we do express. We teach others how to behave to us, how to react to us, by our own degree of Self-acceptance. Others have nothing else to go by. If there are those in our life who are always criticizing us, why are they there except for the reason that we have taught them that we will accept criticism. We always receive what we are. The Science of Mind is not for the purpose of always keeping everything peaceful and serene. We would soon be bored if that happened. This science is for the purpose of moving us into action, into the expression of our great belief in our Self. We must remember that our every experience is made up of our own choice.

When we have a high level of Self-esteem, we do not accept or take the abuse of others. Our high degree of Self-acceptance usually does not cause Mind to draw into our life those who will even try to abuse us. Nothing can touch us but that which represents our Self. Should someone try, our Self-esteem can only assert itself and express itself. It is not that we fight others, but we dare to announce what we are all about, what we stand for. We dare to reveal the authenticity of our Self and then we receive the appropriate reaction.

We are always sending out signals of one kind or another. These signals either attract or repel. Mind draws to us that which corresponds. The more we depend upon others rather than our Self, the more we teach others to take charge. The demand should be made upon our own Self rather than upon someone else. How else are we going to know that we are equal to every challenge except by accepting that challenge and going through it? How else are we to direct Mind except by our own Self-expression?

We often teach the people in our lives to depend upon us. Our insecurity does this as means to manipulate others. It gives us a false sense of power. Others never lean upon us unless we teach them to do this. We are here to have a WE experience, to help and bless others, but we cannot do this by teaching them to be leaners rather than givers. Love does not teach leaning. It teaches living out of one's Self.

The woman who complains that it was her job to wake up her husband each morning because he always slept through the alarms, and when she finally got him out of bed he always abused her for doing so, has only herself to blame. If she is teaching him to be dependent upon her, what is going to happen when she is not there? No one needs the abuse of others, unless they do not like themselves.

We can help others to get up on time by letting them sleep if that is what they choose to do. Being late and reaping the consequences will soon cause them to find their own way of being self-reliant. We are here to help others stand on their own two feet, not make them dependent.

It is said that he who travels alone travels the fastest. This is true. However, this does not mean that in order to go further in life we must eliminate people. What this really means is that in order to go further we must live out of our own Self. We must make the demand upon this Self, not upon others. Others willingly give us all the advice we seek, but what we need is our own answer, not theirs. We must let our inner kingdom take care of the details.

People will always be with us. We will always have things in our life. Consciousness must always become form because that is the way Mind works. When we travel alone we are self-reliant. We still love and care for others. We still have meaningful relationships. Being alone means going within our own Self and drawing from within our own answer.

As we are Self-aware, Self-assertive, and Self-accepting, we teach all in our experience what we are all about. They always accept us. If they will not, then they are not right for us and will go elsewhere, which means that they will be with their right people and we are with ours. In being overly solicitous of others for fear of upsetting them, we are teaching them to get upset, to call the shots, to take away our freedom and Self-respect.

When we make the demand upon our own Self, however, we are then fearlessly facing life. We are not afraid of anything or anyone. Those who are afraid of what is "out there," who always stay at home because of the unforeseen, because of what might or might not happen, are living in a prison of the shadows of their mind. They do not realize that the world is always to them what they are to themselves. They do not realize that others always react to our own action. Yes, our reaction can be said to be an action, but it is the action of not being in charge. It is the action of not daring to be one's Self.

The world, for the most part, desires protection, sympathy and love. The world always responds to us, and it always goes along with what we express even though it does not always seem this way. It seeks to attach itself to us. If we permit it, we are enslaved. It is more loving and more creative to teach the world exactly what we are all about by daring to express our integrity and authenticity. When we choose to think for ourselves and demand to be our own Self in action, Mind attracts to us whatever represents this Self-acceptance in action. It cannot do otherwise.

Ernest Holmes tells us in his book, *The Science of Mind*, that Spirit is the Self-Knowing One...the Absolute. Spirit is that part of man which enables him to know his Self. And so, there is within each one of us that Center that is eternally complete, that Presence which has never been ill and can never be ill. As we contemplate this true Self, Mind can only create the forms that correspond. When we are aware of Who and What we truly are, we are automatically free of the Shadows of the Mind that say otherwise. We experience always our point of attention.

In order to go beyond where we are right now, we must contemplate our Self in new and larger ways. This means that we cannot live vicariously through someone else, and we must not permit them to live vicariously through us. It is what we ourselves are doing that counts.

To be the so-called "perfect mother" and do the work that rightfully belongs to our children does not help them nor does it help us. This does not mean that we must not help others or do favors for them now and again, but so many "favors" are not really that at all. So many times we are so busy trying to please others that our own work does not get done. So often we are doing what others should be doing for themselves that our own "gas tank" does not get filled, our own treatments do not get given, or our own book does not get written.

In the ongoing experience of Self-discovery we will not please everyone and we must not even try. Self-discovery does not mean Self-sacrifice. Self-discovery is always an individual experience and no one can do this for us and we cannot do it for someone else. In going further the demand must be made completely upon our Inner Kingdom, upon this Presence within our own Self. The time has come to stop thinking in terms of getting or controlling and, instead, to think about Who and What we really are. There is much more to life than demonstrating more money. There is living to be freed into action. There is the discovery of the potential within our Self awaiting us, and this can only take place when we are Self-aware and we are about the business of expressing this Self. Self-discovery does not come out of treating for more and more things.

When our treatments are based upon the belief that

there is a need to be filled or that there is a desire as yet unsatisfied, we are going completely against Principle. We are dealing with shadows of the mind. When we are avidly looking forward to our good coming to us, we are separate and apart from that Total Self that is our purpose to reveal.

When we are Self-aware and simply observe unfoldment taking place, we are always living enthusiastically and are giving the highest of our Self to all that we do. The Science of Mind is not a mental attempt to make something happen. It is an acknowledgment that we are already complete and then letting that completeness unfold in its own way.

You may say, "But do I not have the right to choose who is going to be my mate, what my job is to be and where I am to live?" The law of our Being automatically does this for us. We are always attracted to and attract to us that which fits and corresponds to our identity, our level of Self-love, and our now Self-expression. Many people come into our lives, not as mates or lovers, but as a reflection of some aspect of our Self. We are asking amiss by praying to get, by outlining who and what. When we acknowledge that we are already complete and then express that completeness, we are no longer going after someone and trying to force them to be in our lives.

Parents so often look at their children as being infantile and unable to make right decisions. They address themselves to incompleteness rather than completeness.

Self-awareness never speaks to a Being outside of the Self, nor does it expect anything from outside of our own Being. It only makes demands upon Itself. It can do this because it defines Itself as already being complete. Treatment is really making the demand upon God, that Presence within us that is forever complete. We must learn to think for ourselves, out of ourselves. When we do this we do not need to lean upon anyone. We can then move into action and express our own power.

There are many opportunities to attend seminars so that in a concentrated way we hear one speaker after another, day in and day out, as they inspire and teach nothing but the Truth. There are those who not only love this experience but wish that they could live in that pattern forever. But if we do not get busy and begin to express what we have awakened to within ourselves we will find ourselves the eternal student rather than being the teacher.

Reading books, listening to or watching tapes, going to lectures, are all fine. They play a part. But the ideas we get from them must become a way of life. We are only as good as the ideas we are living right now. We have the responsibility of choosing ideas of greatness, those ideas that will take us above and beyond where we are right now in life.

When we believe that our good must come to us from someone or something, then we are looking for the person, the job, or the situation through which it can arrive. However, our good comes through what we ourselves are expressing, even though there are people involved. The kingdom of God is within and when we are giving out of this abundance that resides within our Self, the law of our Self attracts into our life the forms of that expression. Our Self is already complete. There is nothing lacking. Too many of us keep thinking about our past mistakes and the things that have already happened to us and so we look at ourselves as being lacking in some way. But that is not the real Self. We can only experience those ideas that we accept and use, and we have the power to choose a greater idea—any idea—about our Self and act as though it were so.

Our desires represent that which we already are. Instead of hoping and wishing that we could have what seems to be lacking, we must identify with those dreams as already being so, as our being that Self that is equal to them. When we identify with NEED, we automatically look outside of our Self—where it is impossible to find. We are never fulfilled when we look to others for our good. People are in our life as reactions to what we are giving and the way that we are giving it. We must let our desires be a signal to use our thought to be Self-aware so that we can give, share and express in a larger way. Everything else is a denial of God, of Who and What we really are.

In much of family life father is the authority figure. It is he who determines what is right for everyone. It is father who always knows best. Since each one of us, however, is an individualization of God, and God is the Source, then each one of us has his own answer and that answer is to be found within the uniqueness of God that each of us is. For any person to claim that he is the wisest, the highest, the best, is a declaration of separation from the Source. It is personalizing, and when we personalize we cut ourselves off in Mind from that Source. Each person has his own answer that is right for him. Even as we acknowledge that God knows best, we must also acknowledge that God is individualized through each of us, therefore each of us has to look within for our answer.

There are other families in which mother is the dominant figure. It is she who ladles out advice, rules, and answers. If this is the rule always and forever, then she is helping to cripple her children. Each child has his or her own answer and must be taught to depend upon their own inner Self so that eventually they can be free of the roles of mother, father, children and function as independent beings.

We are here to help others build their own foundation of Truth, self-sufficiency, of Truth. We do just the opposite, we give advice. Each answer for each of us must come from within.

It is our purpose to help others by being Self-sufficient ourselves and to influence them to do likewise. How can this be done when we always tell others what to do? How can we help them by being angry when they come up with an answer that does not represent our own way? When we acknowledge that God is EVERYWHERE PRESENT and that each and every person, regardless of who they are, is an individualization of God, then we trust God as each and every one. Others may not be aware that their answer is within their own Being. We can help them by speaking to that wholeness that they already are. We can help them turn within by directing their attention, as well as ours, to their Inner Source.

How can father know best when daughter has a completely different identity and needs? She has her own requirements. She is not a replica of dad. This does not mean that she should be permitted to drive the family car at the age of three or be allowed to acquire a live-in boyfriend at the age of twelve. Should she try to have her way in this manner, she is really saying that she does not have a caring network to help her appreciate her Self.

What are we really saying here? We are accepting that what is right for you is not necessarily best for me. What is uniquely right for me may be the worst thing in the world for you. We are not all the same, even if we are in the same family. God cannot be channeled in someone else's direction as if we were telling God what to do. When we acknowledge that God is the reality of All, we let go and let God be whatever It is as the individual the other person is. We cannot come up with God's answer for someone else. God's answer is never the same because God seeks to work through each person in a special way.

When I was trained as a minister, I was told to do certain things in a definite way. These ways had proven valuable and right for my teacher. However, when I tried to apply all of them in my own ministry, in a different city and a different church, many of them did not work. I then began to experiment and develop my own church in order to fulfill the needs of the congregation. My congregation is different from that of another minister. We draw to us those who more or less represent our own consciousness. To autocratically say that each minister must do the same thing in the same way is a denial of God. Even as we help to fulfill the needs of others, we must also be fulfilling our own uniqueness. Our own God Self cannot be denied.

You have an opinion. I have an opinion. These are neither right nor wrong. They simply reflect our Self. Someone else has their own way, but to impose that way upon others is also a denial of God. God never repeats Itself. We are created out of Spirit, out of God. Spirit is the Father. Spirit is the Source. Not Mom and Dad or anyone else. So many people are in jobs they do not really enjoy because they have conformed to what Mom and Dad wanted for them. Millions of people are suffering from the consequences of doing what someone else has decided upon. We each have our own answer, our own talents, our own needs and our own way. We must dare to live out of our own talents, our own needs and our own way. We must dare to live out of our own Self, to go within and come up with our own answer, that answer that comes from the Mind of God and not out of someone else's insecurity or fear. That someone else is insecure when he or she attempts to impose their beliefs upon us. They are revealing their need to control, dominate, to have someone else agree with them.

Punishment never really works. It is something we impose upon someone else because they do not agree with us. I am not referring to the discipline of a child here. We often refuse to help someone else because he or she has not come through in the way that we have desired. We fail to realize, then, that the people in our life can only be themselves. We have no interest in finding out what they are really all about. All we know is that we expect them to be like us. Our caring expression for others must take into consideration their uniqueness. We do not know what is best for others, sad as that may seem to be. They do not know what is best for us. It is even sadder when we think that they do. Guidance is an individual experience, and guidance comes from within, not without.

What was right for Dad thirty years ago cannot possibly be right for us today. It would not have been right for us then. What is right for us today is within our Self today. No one else knows what it is, no one else has it for us.

We must help others to build their own foundation of Self-awarness by causing them to go within their own Self and coming up with their own answer. Even if it seems illogical to us. Not only does this help them, but it also helps cause us to go within for our own answers. It can be a very wonderful experience when we listen to others and observe their uniqueness, when all the while we are seeking neither agreement nor support.

In conversations we often leap ahead so that we can try to convince them that they don't quite have it all together, while we ourselves do. People think what they think. We are not required to agree. Should they try to convince us that we are wrong, we must realize that they are thinking out of their own uniqueness and this does not say anything against us. We must go on caring and building our relationship by appreciating the specialness that we ourselves are, and that they are as well.

We can know the Truth. We can live the Truth. But is is the Truth that we ourselves are knowing and living that becomes our own experience. If others are receptive to that Truth that we are living then they are set free as well. To try to inflict that Truth upon someone else can only create conflict. Mind is everywhere present and so the Truth that we are living blesses all, as long as we do not try to outline and direct Mind to heal someone or improve them.

If we have a purpose, and all of us do, and if our purpose is not being fulfilled, what is standing in the way? It can only be that we ourselves are not living that Truth of our Being. It can only be that we misinterpret our purpose and are trying to get rather than to BE. Let go of the motivation to get and share instead. The impass, the roadblocks, are simply shadows of the mind. They are a belief that there is power in someone or some thing that is controlling us. It is what we LIVE that counts. It is WHAT WE LIVE that directs Mind.

Our ultimate goal, then, must be not the demonstration of things and people, but the living of the Truth. When we live that Truth, then Truth begins to feed us, to nourish us, to guide and direct our way. The Soul, the subjective part of Mind, can only give to us those ideas, thoughts, and guidance that support the idea that we are living. Out of subjective Mind comes all that we need to know. Our answer is within our Self because Mind is within us and we are within Mind.

We must ask ourselves not "what is it that I can get or have?" but, rather, "what is it that I can give to this moment? What Truth is it that I am to live and reveal right now?" Our goal must be to live in, through and AS God. When we do this, Mind responds and fills our consciousness with those Truths that support this purpose.

If we try to use Truth in order to bring about a healing, our motivation is incorrect. If we try to use Truth and yet hang on to that concept of Self that needs, then we are simply trying to get something rather than to BE something.

To mouth all kinds of statements that are positive and yet not live them is sheer hypocrisy. We have all heard leaders present the principles of Truth, of the Science of Mind, and we have been fascinated by the power of those ideas. Yet we have also seen those same leaders act in ways as though they had never heard of the principles that they are presenting. They teach freedom, yet try to deny freedom to others. They teach love, yet dominate, control and possess the people in their lives. They set up all kinds of rules and regulations that others must follow.

The principles of freedom, love, prosperity and health are all the same. They demand that they be lived at all times. Truth is not something that you can try to serve on Sundays and then forget about during the rest of the week. It is what you are living NOW that counts, that directs Mind, that causes something to change "out there." In LIVING the Truth we must let go of what others are doing and put our whole attention on our own living, our own expression of this Truth.

We so often become discouraged when nothing is happening in our lives. That is because we lay more stress upon what we want to have rather than the living of the Truth. Or, we do our very best to live that Truth, but we still do not seem to demonstrate the forms of it. If we can be so easily discouraged, this can only mean that we have not fully arrived at that point where we ARE the Truth. To go further in life we must more completely surrender the results...we must give ourselves up to BEING the Truth.

When challenges come along, as they must, we should see each and every one as a Divine opportunity to express, reveal and live the Truth—that God is the only power. Without the challenges we may never really prove to ourselves that we have great power within our Self. We must arrive at that point where we are no longer taking thought for our life, for what we can get, for how we would like things to turn out.

Do not use the Truth to avoid anything. Use it simply to be aware of the wholeness that already is, that each of us eternally is. Use it simply to BE. Truth never permits us to run away. It causes us to face life and to live. The Truth has the answer, but the answer is there for us only in the living of that Truth.

The power of success is in BEING rather than in getting. BEING is where the Presence of God is. We must seek no longer to use the Truth but to let the Truth use us. This present moment can be filled with the living of love, beauty, order, success, health and abundance. When we do this, Mind must create the forms of our expression. Mind cannot say no.

CHAPTER V

Learn
to
Love

So many of us hope to form permanent relationships with others, particularly in marriage. We fail to learn by previous experience that the only creative basis for any relationship is love.

Love is that which blesses, inspires, and opens a way for the relationship to unfold and move forward. Yet instead of love, most relationships are based upon sex, physical attraction, the getting of attention, pity, having someone take care of us, the need for security, romance, or the desire to be pampered. None of these is love. They are the exact opposites of love. Love is the eternal giving of the highest of one's self to each and every moment. It demands nothing in return. It expresses for the sake of expressing.

We have all embarked upon relationships thinking that this is love, only to find ourselves in trouble as we go along. And we have chosen to form a relationship with someone who has no knowledge of what love is all about. Where love is not actively being expressed there can only be the experience of whatever it is that we are expressing.

Someone said to me recently, "I want more than

118

anything in the world to be married again. I want to know the experience of love." Marriage, however, does not necessarily bring love. Too many of us make marriage the goal rather than love. They are not synonymous. Marriage should be a result of love, an opportunity in which to express love in a continuing and expanding way. Infatuation does not last. It is quickly gone. Yes, it can be a lot of fun, or it can mean a great deal of heartache. But it still has nothing to do with love.

Love is that which creates an ongoing, joyous, challenging and exciting relationship. Love is that which opens the door to communication. It is that which blesses, heals, and shows the way. It doesn't, however, just happen. It has got to be learned. It has got to be developed. It must be expressed. Prejudice, hate and judgment are learned. So does love have to be taught and learned by us all.

We cannot really live that to which we do not dedicate ourselves. If love is to be the center of our life, then there must right now be a complete dedication to love. Whatever we dedicate ourselves to, Mind finds a way to fulfill. Mind must provide the answers, the way, and the results. It is never too late. Anyone can begin right now, no matter what their situation in life. Within every dedication is the Intelligence and the Power of the universe that knows how to fulfill that dedication. Mind always provides the way to open into the expression of love, the completeness, that resides within us all.

The best way to learn how to love is to be taught by our parents, our teachers, the authority figures in our life. But since most of them have never been taught how to love, they are not usually examples of what love is all about. They are always busy trying to discipline, to take charge of all of our behaviors, so that they forget that the way in which they are acting is the way that they are teaching. For the most part they are trying to prove themselves, to make us agree with their viewpoint. They do not realize that the people in their world have their own answers, and their own uniqueness to discover and express.

Love is the joyous expressing of our own Self-acceptance, and then helping others to do the same thing. The moment that someone else dares to think for himself, we become uneasy if we are not Self-aware and living out of the authority of our own Self.

Our teachers, for the most part, have not radiated love, enthusiasm and joy themselves, therefore they have not awakened within us our own joy of being. We now must turn elsewhere to learn how to love. The only place that we can really turn to with complete success is within our own Self.

Now that we are aware that everything and everyone in our experience is but a shadow of the mind, of our own consciousness, we can release them all and dedicate ourselves to love. What we ourselves express is what we ourselves are individually going to experience. No one else can do this for us. As we dedicate ourselves to love in a conscious way, we receive from within ourselves the ways to express and reveal love.

When love is the purpose, the goal, then love can infuse our every moment. It is up to us to fill each moment with the love that is already within us. Everything in our life has the essence, the personality, the nature, of our Self. It is our true purpose in life to fill each moment with love. No one else will do this for us. It is always the law of life that what we give is what we have.

Many people believe that love is sex, and therefore love is something only to be shared with the sexual partner. But love and sex are two entirely different things. Sex can be infused with love, as can anything else, but not vice versa, for love is what you radiate regardless of who is in your experience, no matter where you are. We can have exciting and rewarding relationships without sex.

The more that we fill each and every moment with love, with communication, with sharing, the more every area of our life is rich and complete. Communication is a sending out, a giving, to whoever is in our now experience. We can have a relationship of love with plants, with animals, with the things in our life. I am even now sharing, or communicating with you by means of this book. I am giving something from within my Self and you are responding, corresponding, and reflecting that which I am expressing. Without the expression of love, our time is really wasted. Without love, we give the least of ourselves rather than the most.

We must always remember that we are forever directing Mind in every moment of every day. Mind must create what we continually feed into it. If we are not giving and expressing love, then we are revealing something else and Mind cannot say no. There is nothing more healing, more rewarding or exciting than the expression of love. What love touches begins to bloom, to open up, to flower. Love, however, is not what someone else is expressing. It must be what we ourselves are NOW revealing.

Let us stop blaming the people in our world for doing the only thing they know how to do—which is to be themselves. In our active acknowledgment and recognition that love is the nature of our Self, and of all in our lives, we can begin right now to give, to share, to radiate this fullness that is already within us and to let Mind take care of the results.

We are so often fighting the shadows of our mind by trying to change and improve ourselves, to overcome something, to get something, and these shadows are

121

forever controlling us. Since there is always an outpicturing of what goes on within our thought, let us put our now attention where it really belongs. The only important purpose in our life is the revealing of love, of our True Self. As we do this, Mind automatically creates the forms of our expression. The forms are all that happens to us.

Very often we get caught up with the challenge of procrastination. We have gotten into the habit of putting off until tomorrow, or even later, what we should be doing today. As a result, we have become so swamped with a backlog of work that it seems impossible to ever be free. This is a result of living at the level of effect and not living in the Now. When we are busy expressing love through all that we do, we are so excited about doing whatever we are doing that we accomplish each task as it comes along.

When we are at one with the idea of living eternally in the Now, then we are the activity of accepting every challenge that comes to us AS it comes along. It is the law of Mind that is bringing to us the outpicturing of our Self right now and Now is when the challenge is meant to be accepted and gone through. When the bill comes to us is the time it is meant to be paid. When the letter comes to us is when it is meant to be answered. When we notice that something needs to be done is the time that we should do it.

When we are living in this fashion we are always free of the debt of yesterday and we never have the problem of forgetting. Our Self is always prepared. It can do anything. We always have every answer within us. Procrastination is the result of not trusting our Self, of feeling insufficient to the task at hand. But when we choose to believe in our Self, then that choice causes Mind to guide us accordingly.

When we think that we are too tired we are only using

an idea that results in putting off. The law of our own Being, however, has brought the opportunity to us, which means that we have the energy, the courage, the answer, whatever is required, to handle the challenge right here and now. It is much easier to live in the Now than to have to face our Self-hate, Self-rejection, for letting things go, for identifying with the idea of procrastination.

Labels always get in the way. They are shadows of the mind. We must take everything that goes with the labels we place upon ourselves. All of the previous experience of each label, all that we have ever heard about that label, now controls us. In saying to ourselves that we are a procrastinator, Mind finds ways to fulfill that choice, that idea. The way to move beyond this is take the ideal idea and move with it. "I handle every challenge as it comes along. I live in the now and do all that needs to be done as it needs to be done."

When we face the challenges that come along right then and there we soon find ourselves free of yesterday's work and there are no longer mountains of work that should have been taken care of long ago. We can be so organized with our work that we get it all sorted out into emergencies, not so serious, take care of later, etc. that we never do anything. We spend all of our time organizing. But when we handle it as it comes along we are free of it forever. There is that within each of us that knows how to do what needs to be done. Even if we cannot complete it all right now because necessary information has to be obtained, at least we can do something to get it going.

We all have our lessons to learn and each time we procrastinate we learn that this does not work. We learn the pain of not living in the now.

We must ask ourselves, "Am I showing forth the highest of my Being, the highest that God is capable of

doing as me?'' If not, it is only because we have chosen
to live a lesser idea. If there is disorder in our lives, it
is because we have chosen to express disorder. If order
is what we want to have, then order is what we must
choose to express. We learn to love by choosing to love.
We learn to live by choosing to live. We learn to establish
order by revealing order in what we are doing right now.
WE ONLY HAVE WHAT WE ARE NOW EXPRESSING.

Living in the now is one of the most exciting ways of
life. We are always on top of everything. We are always
free because we have gotten into the habit of doing
today's work today.

When we are Self-aware—which is acknowledging our
True Being, our ideal—we never have any fear of disease
or of anyone because everything in our experience is
created out of our active awareness of this ideal. We are
free to agree with our adversaries and to do it quickly
because we know that the only power in our life is the
power of our individual Self.

Nothing can touch us that is outside of our own consciousness. When we are centered within our Self, we
can truly begin to love. When we have chosen to accept
our own Self as the power in our life we can really begin
to help others to think for themselves, to live out of their
own inner resources.

When we are insecure, however, we must always try
to get others to agree with us. We must always try to
make sure that no one is getting away with a thing. In
believing that others are cause to our experience we get
caught up in blaming and fighting them, rebelling, and
thus we are never free. Our need to have others agree
with us indicates the use of a very limited identity. Mind
can only create and draw into our experience whatever
represents that identity.

We must always agree with our adversary because one

of our great purposes is to help others to think for themselves. We are here to recognize that God is the only power and that God is individualized by each and every person everywhere, regardless of what appears to be.

We are not bound by what we thought, said or did yesterday. We are only bound by what we are thinking and doing right now. Many times we are reminded by others of what we said yesterday, and they are holding us to that as if their very life were at stake. They are only holding us to it because they haven't learned how to think for themselves. When they ask us to help make a decision for them we must say to them, "What do YOU think? It is your challenge and the answer must fit you. It is what comes from within your own Self that is truly important."

It is our purpose to not only stand on our own two feet and to think for ourselves, but we are here to help others do the same. In our giving advice we are really trying to take away their own Self-discovery. Each and every one of us must eventually turn to that power within and learn to love and respect that Self. We must agree with our adversary, not only to be free of having to defend our Self, but because in doing so we are respecting their right to think for their own Self, regardless of what their choice is. We only help others by recognizing their sufficiency. We never help them with our advice, our worry or fear. Love makes no attachments or demands. It releases, loses, and respects the self-authority of all.

If we have to prove that we are right and that others are wrong, there is something within our own Self that has to be healed. Each one of us is unique and special. When we know that for ourselves we know it for others as well. We must permit others to be whatever they are. We must accept that each person is an individualization of God and whatever their answer may be, it is theirs and therefore we respect it. We may not agree with their viewpoint, but it is theirs. As long as they do not demand that we conform to it, we must permit them to believe as they believe. In our own expression of Self-love and Self-respect, we must dare to be ourselves. At the same time we must permit others to be what they are. In that way we are simply observing and we are thus free of the anger and frustration that can only come by trying to get others to agree with us.

Agreement is what we give to others, not what we demand of them. In our demanding anything of anyone we have an instant problem. We have lost our freedom to BE. We learn to love by choosing to be our own Self in action. We teach love by demanding of ourselves that we agree with whoever is in our life, by acknowledging their specialness, even though their opinions are the opposite of ours.

It is always ego that demands agreement because ego needs the support of others. We can never demonstrate anything that we demand. Our very demand is an expression of uncertainty and thus this is what we experience. Submission is not agreement and is not healthy, because we are then denying our own person-hood and validity. Each of us must believe in our Self and actively reveal what we are all about. We must help others do likewise.

Our security comes only out of our choosing to believe in our Self and to actively express that Self. When we are doing this we are free to help others do the same. Nothing can touch us but that which represents our con-sciousness and so our real security is to be found in the expression of love.

So many times when we find ourselves in a problem or when there is a negative appearance we immediately

126

begin to protect ourselves from that appearance. The moment we begin to defend ourselves we have lost our freedom. In defending we are really saying that the power in our life is outside rather than within. The truth is that no external thing or person has any power except that which we give it. The power in our experience is our own Self, not someone else.

I am often asked to give treatments for divine protection. I used to do this until I realized what I was actually doing. When I realized that I was contradicting myself when I said that God is the only power and then went on to treat for protection I stopped and have never treated for protection again. If we believe that God is the ONLY power, then there is nothing else. If we believe that there is power in people and things, then this belief becomes our now experience, when all the while it is nothing but a shadow of the mind.

We need never defend ourselves from someone else because in our own experience we are the power. The belief that we have to do something about the appearance is another shadow of the mind. In our own experience all there is is Self. In defending ourselves we are really trying to get something rather than to give. Nothing can touch us except that which reflects that which we are giving.

Every once in a while someone comes to me with great fear in their eyes. They have just been given a medical verdict by a doctor who has looked at the X-rays and has declared that which the person has always feared. But is there power in an X-ray? Certainly not. There is no power in any external thing. Yet the person who has been given the pronouncement caves in and believes that all is lost. Or he or she marshals every resource in fighting that X-ray, or that verdict. Other doctors are brought in and even the practitioner is asked to help overcome this problem. In fighting the problem, however, we are fighting a shadow. An opinion. A belief. However, there is no power in body, in an X-ray, in a verdict, in a shadow. There is power only in our own consciousness, in our own Self. When that Self is identified as being God individualized, there is nothing to fight or to overcome. There is only the realization that the perfection of God is the perfection of the individual.

We have all had the experience of hearing that someone has been talking about us behind our back. They have been gossiping. When we hear about this we usually react. We defend. We attack in return. We plan counter-moves. We begin to fight back by defending ourselves to ourselves first of all. We may write letters, make phone calls, or waylay certain people and defend ourselves in whatever way comes to mind. But all the while we are fighting a shadow. No one has ever really talked about us behind our back. No one has ever talked about us in front of us. Each and every one is talking to himself about himself. What they are saying has nothing to do with us. It is their own consciousness being expressed and revealed.

When we are busy defending ourselves we are saying that we are insecure, that perhaps the other person is right. That defense is instantly accepted into subconscious mind and Mind creates the experience of the defense and so the problem is magnified. That shadow becomes an experience because the defense gives power to it. Nothing can touch us but our own Self. There is no power in body, no power in ANY external thing.

If we have to make sure that everyone in our life likes us, then we have to satisfy or please each and every person we come across. In trying to get every one to approve of us we have to give up our own uniqueness and become like the other person. We have to agree with everything they say and do. This, however, is too restricting upon our own personhood, and leads to all kinds of emotional and physical problems. Even if we say that we do this only for the few special people we love, or THE significant other, we are still assuming that the power in our life is outside of our Self rather than within. No matter how much we love someone, we cannot always agree with or be like him or her.

We are told in the Bible that those who live by the sword shall die by the sword. Yet we fail to realize that so much of our thought is a mental sword. We are mentally fighting, defending, opposing and trying to kill. We always reap the consequences of that approach to life. Consciousness always becomes form.

With the recognition that our Self in our own experience is all there is, there is nothing to fight, nothing to fear. In resisting not evil we are really saying that all there is is love. In not resisting there is only the power of the Self in action. Non-resistance does not mean becoming a doormat. It means simply Being. It means actively revealing what we are all about.

When we live out of our own Self-authority, we dare to BE whatever we are, whatever we have chosen to express. Self-authority means that we fill each and every moment with the greatness of our Ideal Self and let Mind take care of creating the results. We are now an actor rather than a reactor.

In believing in our Self we are affirming that all power is within and that absolutely nothing can touch us but our Self. This means that nothing can be in our life except the forms of our consciousness. When ours is the consciousness of love, then love can be the only experience.

If there seems to be some sort of discord in our life right now, and we are saying to our Self, "How could this possibly happen to me?", we've got to realize that the law of our Self is always in action. There is only one law, and it is the law of Mind. Mind always creates whatever corresponds to our Self. But what about the law of love, the law of life, the law of Truth, the law of God? What about all of these different laws? There is still only one law—the law of Mind—and it is always directed by our identity—our state of mind—whether we are using Truth, love, hate, anger or whatever.

When our Self is filled with love, then love is the consciousness that becomes form. When we are at one with the Presence of God, then this is the nature of our Self, and God fills our experience. But we always live out of the law of our Self.

Fear, anxiety, anger and love are not to be found out in the world in our own experience. They are all within our own Self. Thus, if discord is in our life, we have somehow violated the law of love. The world is not doing anything to us. We are experiencing anger only because we have failed to consciously acknowledge the perfection of our Being.

If we have ever looked to greener pastures, wishing that we were elsewhere because where we were was not ideal, we have not been actively acknowledging our True Self. Whenever we got to where we thought we would be happy, we then wished that we were back where we came from. This again says that we are not filling the Now with the highest of our Self. We always have what we are giving to the present moment, no matter where we are.

We so often await with dread the results of our mistakes of yesterday to catch up with us. Knowing that the law of cause and effect is always in action and must bring us our just desserts, we anticipate the worst because of yesterday's less than ideal thought and deed. But the fact is that we are not bound by yesterday's mistakes unless we are still living them. We are bound only by what we are NOW living, giving, revealing and expressing. How absolutely great to realize that all there is is the NOW, that yesterday is gone and that all we need do is identify with the law of Love, of God, right now. Instantly we are then free.

So-called instantaneous healings can and do take place when we let go of yesterday's shadows because Mind creates the consequences of what we are knowing in the present moment. I believe that each one of us is already whole, perfect and complete. When we accept that, instead of the shadows, opinions and beliefs of others, Mind causes body to correspond. Body always responds because Mind cannot say no. In essence, then, we do not need to be healed because we are already whole. Our thinking needs to be changed. We need to release the shadows and become at one with "I Am" ideas of perfection.

We are always hearing complaints about the high cost of living. People often move to other locations because it is supposed to be cheaper there. That is just a shadow of the mind, however, because we still live under the law of the Self. When we identify with abundance, abundance is the nature of the Self and we have all that we require as it is needed. We have all in our world that reflects the consciousness of our own Self.

Things are not more safe and free elsewhere unless we take with us a strong, loving and vital Self. We cannot suddenly leap from where we are to where we want to be and when we get there begin to be that strong, vital and loving Self. We must begin being it where we currently are. Running away is never the answer. We have to learn to love in our present situation because if we don't do it here, we won't do it there. Being our True Self in action where we presently are is the only answer. Everything in our life is created out of that Self. That Self is ALREADY whole and complete. We need only realize it. We need only live it, express it, reveal it, in whatever we are doing, regardless of where we are. Mind must cause body and experience to correspond.

Whenever we sit in judgment upon our Self, we are looking back at yesterday. Yesterday is any time previous to the present moment. This judgment can only cause us to now experience that judgment, even though it may seem to be the judgment of someone else. If we have accepted it, we are using it. In using it, we experience the consequences.

If we are depressed, it is still a shadow of the mind becoming form. The depression is still created out of our violating the law of love. We become depressed because we depend upon someone. We look to them for our good. We see them as being the power in our life for good or bad and thus we feel that there is nothing we can do about them. We believe them to be all-powerful. True, we cannot do anything about someone else. But we can do something. We can choose to look at our own Self in a positive and creative way.

The moment we accept Who and What we really are and begin acting as though it were so, we no longer are depressed. The moment we express joy and love we no longer have a problem. There is no such thing as a penalty for yesterday's mistake. Today is all we have. Mind is creating out of what we NOW believe our Self to be.

We can find a tragedy to get upset about if there is not already one in our life. Our we can find something to be joyous about. We have the power of choice. We are literally creating our experience out of what we choose to think and feel. We have this power always to make our own decisions and to take the responsibility for what we think. Regardless of what has already happened in our lives, we can be free of all of those shadows by making some creative choices. We have to learn to love, to love our Self, no matter what that Self has been. It is what it IS that counts.

We do not learn to love by going on a diet. We go on a diet by learning to love. We do not become thin by thinking thin. We can image the skinniest of bodies, but if we do not love our Self, we are going to find ways to punish our Self. We see all sorts of people jogging all over the cityside and countryside these days. Some are doing it as an action of loving the Self. Most, however, are puffing away because they have compared their bodies with those of others. Many are scared out of their wits by their doctors having told them that they must exercise or they will die. Exercise is necessary, but if we are doing it for the wrong reasons, it is not really going to help us at all. If we love our Self, that Self takes creative action that is constructive for body and every area of life. If we do not love our Self, then no matter what we do to improve body will be a waste for Mind will find some other way in which to punish our Self.

We build consciousness by choosing ideas of greatness and identifying with them, by expressing them. We learn to love by being involved with the active expression of our Ideal Self. We cannot help but eat, act, live or feel except in ways that reflect our level of Self-love, Self-respect. All that we do reveals our Self. All habit patterns are created out of our degree of Self-esteem or Self-rejection. Diet or exercise is simply something that we do according to how we feel about our Self. Stuffing ourselves with food and not doing any kind of exercise are simply signals that we do not really like ourselves.

We build consciousness by selecting great ideas and living those ideas. We build consciousness by choosing to love our Self, regardless of what we have already done. We build consciousness by identifying with our Ideal Self and revealing it no matter where we are. We learn to love by being involved with this on-going expression of our God Self. In choosing to love our Self we no longer seek ways of causing torment to our Self. All of our habit patterns are created out of whatever level of Self-esteem we have decided to have.

We have all had the experience of saying that after the first of the year we are going to go on a diet, stop smoking, drinking, begin a strenuous program of exercise. The New Year arrives and before long it is June and we still haven't gotten started. Our yearnings for what we desire are reflections of a starved and incomplete sense of Self. What we say we are going to do we probably never will, otherwise we wouldn't say it. It is what we are now doing that reveals what we are.

Give up the desire for a more perfect body. Give up the need to compare ourselves with others and instead begin to build the consciousness of love for ourselves and others. Actively acknowledge our Ideal Self and let It live through all that we think and do in the present moment.

Our happiness is not dependent upon acquiring a larger and more beautiful home. What is required is a higher concept of Self. The home automatically corresponds.

Many people put a great deal of their money into their clothes. They worship clothes, feeling that these garments will make them beautiful, desireable and more complete. But clothes have no power. One can be beautifully and appropriately dressed, but what good is that if we are not expressing love? It is love that counts. Clothes are but a shadow of the Mind. The more we love our Self the more beautifully we are dressed, but the clothes are then just an extension of our consciousness. We select them, put them on and forget about them as we move into the expression of love.

When we put full attention upon body, we may love

our Self today and hate that Self tomorrow. In dealing at the level of effect we will waver all over the place in this experience of Self. However, we are not our body. We are our Self. Just as the people who love us today may hate us tomorrow because we do not agree with them, so we cannot count on others, nor can we count on body.

Count on your Self. Count on this True Self, this Ideal Self, that you really are. We must always remember that power is within our own consciousness, never anywhere else. We can reveal this Ideal Self in any moment and we can begin right where we are. In expressing the qualities and energy of this Ideal, we have a sense of completeness, fullness. We are automatically free of trying to stuff ourselves with food or add to our Self with a constant stream of things.

We can take a statement, an affirmation, and repeat it over and over again. The repeating of it does not make it so, although the stating of it does indeed remind us that this idea is already so. However, the stating of it does not make it so. It is already so. Saying over and over again, "The sun is shining," does not make it shine. It just makes us aware that it is shining. It is not the purpose of any affirmation to make something happen. The affirmation does not create God. God already is. It does not create health. Health already is because God already is.

The Truth does not bring about a healing. It reminds us that we are already perfect, and this realization simply becomes form. The realization acts upon Mind and Mind causes body to correspond. The affirmation acknowledges a particular good and we then must move it into expression. It is the action of the idea that proves that we believe.

To use our thought to try to create something can only take us away from the truth that our good already IS.

Yes, our point of attention always becomes visible. But having our attention upon what we want is causing Mind to keep it from us because we are really saying that our good is not already so. When we try to get something rather than live something we become frustrated because we only have what we live. The power is not in the treatment, the word, but in the Self, in the Presence. The treatment merely reminds us of Who and What we already are. We are then free to act as though it were so. We must actually express that Self that already IS. We have whatever it is that we express.

We listen to an opera star sing an aria. Or we respond to our favorite pop singer singing one of our favorite songs. That singer is not creating the song. The song already is. The song is within the consciousness of the singer. He or she can create excitement that we tune into, but the song already is. Even the one who writes the song is merely tuning in to that which already is. They are the avenue through which the song comes forth.

We are all expressing something that is already within us. It is revealed through our uniqueness, our individuality. We merely remind ourselves that it is there. The reminding does not create. It permits expression. Within all of us is the wholeness, perfection and completeness that we call God. It already is. Health already is, and so is abundance, love, and energy. When we remind ourselves of these aspects of our Being, we reveal them and Mind causes body to correspond.

When we are aware of our Complete Self and express that Self with love and authority, then Mind simply causes the outer to reflect the inner. There is power in thought, but the Self is the real power. Thought does not create. It reminds. Mind then creates.

Some people feel that they have no reason to live, that they do not have any purpose in life, that they have no one to live for. This is their experience only because they are looking outside of their Self for their good. They are looking to someone, or to some thing. There is always a reason to live when we are permitting this Ideal Self to reveal Itself through us. We have mistakenly come to believe that we are here to receive...or that the power in our lives is "out there" as someone or some thing. But we are here to let something out. To give, to share.

When we remind ourselves of that complete Self that we ALREADY are, that we are God's means to love, to live, to express, and then begin expressing that sense of completeness, there can be no depression. We find all kinds of reasons, then to live, to be a blessing to the people in our lives. We must continually remind ourselves, however, of this Presence, of this Truth of our Being. When we do this life is an exciting adventure and we are soon living spontaneously in the present moment rather than demanding that everything happen exactly in the way that we want it to happen.

When we believe that thought is power and then use it to try to make something happen, we demonstrate frustration and anger. This happens because Mind can only create out of what we are now expressing. If we are not living love, how can Mind create an experience of love, or draw into our lives someone to receive and reflect that love? In mentally forcing something to happen we become irritated and that irritation becomes visible in our experience, or in our bodies.

In letting go of the fighting of the shadows of the mind and instead revealing the qualities of the Total Self, every area of our life is blessed and so are the people in our world. Easter is not for the purpose of reminding us of a certain man who lived nearly two thousand years ago, but of Who and What we already are. The Christ is that Total Self, God individualized, that ALREADY is. When we live it our days are so filled with opportunities and expressions of joy and love that our life is filled to overflowing.

We often see couples who, as the years go along, seem to drift apart. They separate and go their own way. Is that bad? Is it good? No. It just is. It usually indicates that one is growing in Self-awareness while the other is not. Or that both are growing, but in different directions. Because of our belief that society is a power and that we must do what it wants us to do, many women tie themselves to the home and cease to seek opportunities to use their talents in greater ways, in newer ways. The person being out in the world accepts the challenges that come along and discovers more about the potential of the inner Self. We may be sad to see someone is leaving his or her mate, yet it is not for us to judge. It is just that their different levels of consciousness no longer permit them to share their lives.

In learning to love we must set the people in our lives free so that they can stand on their own feet, and we must demand of others that we be permitted to do the very same. To most people the meaning of a friend is someone who agrees with you, who has the same points of view. But that is not necessarily friendship. Yes, the law of attraction draws into our experience those who help us fulfill our Self. However, this does not mean that we are all exactly the same. Fulfillment does not mean that we get comfortable and begin to stagnate. Stagnation can only take place when we have "yes" people around us, those who say that they agree even when they do not.

Life is an unfolding experience and therefore we have to be receptive to new and greater ideas, to a greater expression of our inner resources. Having people around us who make us feel eternally comfortable is a way to stop that unfoldment. A true friend is someone who supports our uniqueness and our greatness and will not settle for our being anything less than the potential of our Self in action. He or she demands the right to fulfill their own uniqueness as well.

If we are insecure in ourselves, we want someone who will give us sympathy, love and understanding. But love and understanding do not perpetuate our feeling sorry for ourselves. Each one of us is special, and this specialness must be attained and maintained. If we are to have carbon copies of our Self around us all the time, there is no uniqueness. We are not here to have clones in our life. We are here to live from within our own Self, and to help others live out of their own inner kingdom as well.

Learning to love is learning to let go of others, to cease leaning, and to dare to be one's own Self. So many people get married for the wrong reasons. Those reasons cause them to stop growing. Our purpose cannot be to have others agree with us. We must learn to think for ourselves and to help others do the same. Arguments are the result of each of us demanding that the other give up his uniqueness and surrender to the power of the other. But that is not love.

In communiation there should certainly be good, healthy discussions of what each is all about. There should be the free expression of the unique Self. But love makes no demands upon the other to give up anything. In learning to love we must be willing to accept every opportunity that comes along to grow, to live out of our own Self in a greater way.

I have often received mail from people who blame me for their problems. They say that I have told their friends or loved ones to stop giving money, help, and support to them, and now they are desperate because they do not know where to turn. However, I never tell others what to do. What they do must come out of their own

Self. If they are demanding that others no longer lean upon them, then they are just taking a stand to help others realize that we can only really count on our own Self.

No one can ruin the life of someone else. No one can take away the good of someone else. These are choices we make for ourselves. Each and every one is simply experiencing his own consciousness. If a problem is at hand, the opportunity has arrived to begin taking responsibility for our own experience, for our own reaction, for our own life.

Each of us has to eventually learn that our good resides within our own Self. Within that Self are untold resources and riches. Friendship is helping others to demonstrate their own home, their own money, their own health by the acknowledgment of their own inner power. None of these can really be dispensed by someone else. We have to individually earn our good by right of consciousness.

There is always an answer for every challenge. For each of us that answer is within our own Self. There must be an ongoing experience of unfoldment if we are to be happy, free and self-sufficient. Whoever helps us to do that is a friend, a true friend. Anyone we can lean upon for everything being provided us is not a real friend. Anyone who tries to tell us what to do is not a friend. Those who throw the ball back to us and ask, "What do YOU really think?" is helping us to turn within our own Self and to come up with a unique answer that can serve our own specialness. Mind is always creating opportunities for our Self to be fulfilled, and there is ingrained within our Self that true greatness that we really are.

A genius is someone who dares to listen from within his Self, who dares to be his Self, regardless of how he differs from the common herd. So much of television is geared for the common denominator. It is after ratings, and the way to get highest rating is to please the most people. It therefore comes out as a formula that has proven successful before, but now shows no spark of originality, specialness or courage. Courage is daring to be true to the integrity of one's Self. The more we think for ourselves, the more we hear the voice of our True Self.

Groups of people may accomplish certain things by working together, but they are usually led by someone who is listening to his or her inner voice. Life, however, is not a group experience. In being bound by the group, we have to agree with it. We must surrender our own inner beat to be in harmony with the common chord. There is nothing wrong with having people in our lives, even groups of people, but we must maintain our own integrity and be forever true to our Self.

The expression of love makes no demands in the way of receiving, but it does make demands upon the individual Self, upon the Presence of God being individualized through each and every one.

CHAPTER VI

We are Universal

We are not just bodies filling up space. We are not just bodies and the activity of those bodies in a certain place at a certain time. We are infinitely more than that. The reality of our Self functions in Consciousness, and since Consciousness is in Mind and Mind is everywhere present, then what we are is an activity in Mind that is not bound by the outlines of form. Mind is everywhere present and since we are an expression within Mind, then we are everywhere present. *We are Universal.*

To believe that we are confined to a place is but a shadow of the mind, a belief that causes us to function within the limits of that belief. All the while we are Consciousness, which is everywhere present.

When we are in the midst of some activity, the activity of our Self, our purpose—if someone should come into our thought during that activity, we must realize that they have come to us out of Universal Mind because our consciousness has attracted him or her to us. They are there for a purpose. It is not for us to be involved with them at the level of a problem. It is for them to be at one with the Truth that we ourselves are knowing and living.

In our experience of freedom from all limitation, in our being free of the shadows of the mind, it is our purpose to use only those ideas that are positive and up. Should we think of those people at the level of their problems, we are not helping either them or ourselves.

People do come to mind, into our use of thought, and there is certainly nothing wrong with that. We can only bless others, however, by knowing and living the Truth—those ideas that produce love, health, wealth and success. Since our thinking is everywhere present, this knowing and living helps us to see them as nothing less than an individualization of God. The Truth that we know blesses them wherever they are.

Since we are Universal, then they are Universal as well, and since God is everywhere present, then they are with us in thought solely for the purpose of benefiting by the Truth. They have come to mind either because they have tuned in to our consciousness or because our consciousness has attracted them so that we can be a living example of Truth for them. This Truth is then brought alive within their consciousness and is experienced in whatever way is uniquely right for them. That Truth is not only a blessing to them, but to ourselves as well, and whoever else is within our consciousness. *We are Universal* and all that we think and do, and the way that we do it, is potentially a great blessing to all the world.

There is One Mind, and that Mind is Universal. All people, all things, reside within that One Mind. Within that Mind is all thought—all who think, all ideas, all that has ever been thought or will ever be thought. More importantly, it includes all that is NOW being thought. This Universal Mind is our unique means to communicate with each other, to be at one with each other. You and I are always sending thought into Mind and receiving from it. We are a way of thought, an identity, a conciousness. We, being a thinking and feeling being, an expressing Self, are touching the Universe through this magnificent instrument of Mind.

Whoever turns to us in thought, in consciousness, to our level of Self-awareness and Self-expression, does so for a purpose. It is for the purpose of being lifted up and beyond their problem or to share in our level of thought. Whoever tunes in to our plateau of consciousness is supported by this way of thought. Mind instantly acts to create, to cause body to correspond or to express through them the integrity of our Being. This does not mean that we are coercing anyone or that we are demanding that they do exactly what we are doing or that they must think exactly what we are thinking.

The people in our consciousness are still unique expressions and avenues of Life, and that uniqueness is always going to be theirs, unless they unwittingly give it up. In our knowing the Truth, we are not dealing with the shadows of world belief or the way that we think they should live their lives.

When we are using the science of mind to "get" rather than to reveal, we are going against the nature of Life, we are not fulfilling our reason for Being. We are not here to benefit our own lives materially, although that automatically happens when we live out of the Total Self. We are here to tune in to a way of thought, a level of thought, and to let It shine through all that we think, say and do. Our purpose is a universal one, rather than a selfish one. We are not here to live for ourselves, but THROUGH our Self.

When our motivation is that of sending out, then the universality of our nature is truly in action and is a great blessing to all.

We must not live selfishly. We are universal and this world cannot afford our anxieties, our fears, our depressions or our unhappiness. There is a way to be free of all of that so that we are able to be about the business of doing our work, of giving creatively to all. That way is through the realization that there is no power in effect. The power is only in cause.

In the realization that we are already complete....that we are living out of a Source, a Self, that is God individualized....then we must realize that our purpose is to give and not to receive, even though the receiving corresponds to the giving. We are here to be a blessing to every person who comes into our use of thought.

When someone comes to mind, know that it is for the divine purpose of our lifting up by means of Truth—the Truth of Being. Instead of worrying about them or reinforcing their problem, use those ideas that will free them. We don't have to outline it all for them by insisting that they behave in the way that we want them to behave. Release the person and simply acknowledge that God is the only power, that the allness of God is everywhere present and forever in expression. Then let that idea shine through all that we ourselves are now doing. There being one Mind, this person who comes to mind must benefit by the power of our knowing, of our doing. Whether someone comes to mind who lives in Italy, Johannesburg, Chicago or Mexico City, it does not matter. *We are Universal*, Mind is Universal, and that Truth that we know is EVERYWHERE PRESENT.

Whatever our thought is, it is affecting our Self first of all. It being in our own consciousness, the law of Mind takes it into the infinite subconscious Mind and touches every area of our own being first of all. Even though we seem to be thinking of someone else, we are doing so through our own identity, our own consciousness and so we ourselves are always affected.

Those who come to mind are a divine opportunity for

us to know the Truth and thus free them to that Truth as well as our own Self.

If we are thinking of someone in a limited way, such as judging them or going over their problem, not only does that not help them, it does not help us. If we use an idea of poverty, disease, failure or weakness about them, we are still using an idea in our own consciousness. Whatever we see or hear is within OUR consciousness. It is our own interpretation of that which is really there, and that interpretation may not be correct. It may be a shadow of the mind.

If God is all there is, and this we must accept if we are to be free of doubt and fear, then whatever we see or hear in the way of limitation is not the Truth. It is an illusion. It is a shadow of the mind, of our own use of thought. If we are using these shadows, then we do not really believe that God is all there is. The Truth is that God is all there is, and thus every person everywhere is God individualized, regardless of what appears to be. We must know the Truth in order to live freely, and to be a blessing to all in our consciousness.

Should we be giving our attention to any mediocre or small idea, then we are the ones to reap its consequences. Our use of thought is eternally creating for us. If others are receptive to our way of thought, then it is also creating for them.

Our thought is tremendously powerful because it is universal. It is everywhere because Mind is everywhere. Each person in our life represents a divine and glorious opportunity for us to know the Truth so that they are richly blessed by these ideas of greatness that we are using. No one needs or deserves our criticism or condemnation. They are there to receive our recognition of sufficiency, of the intelligence and power of the Total Self. As we use thoughts of success, health, wealth and love, then we are released to our own ongoing purpose of revealing and living those ideas while the people in our lives are released in our thought to whatever life is doing through them.

Others are not meant to stay in our thought. They enter our thought to go out of our thought. When they stay there, we are, in essence, mentally manipulating them. This can only hurt us. All of the people in our lives want and need to be free to go about their own business. Their business is that of revealing their Total Self, that which God is seeking to express through them. Each and every one! Even these people are shadows of the Mind because the Reality of our life is God as us.

If we see people as being in our lives in order to give to us, we are going in the wrong direction. Our true and most creative direction is to give, not to get. Receiving is always equal to the giving.

The people we feel obligated to we do not like. And so it is with each of them. Our gifts of love must have no strings attached. We cannot decide how others are to live their lives or how they are to unfold. The only way we can live creatively is to give each other the freedom to experience our own potential.

Freedom does not mean that we are going to be alone or that we have to live alone. The law of attraction is always in action, bringing into our experience whoever or whatever represents our own consciousness, our level of giving. But each of us must be free to live out life as our own uniqueness, whatever that may be. If others are always downgrading our dreams and goals, then we must not share those dreams and goals with them because they feel threatened by them. Share them only with those who believe in themselves and are already fulfilling their dreams.

Our loved ones come into our thought for us to release

them to their own expressions of success, not for us to manipulate them into what we want them to do.

It is a great burden to carry people in consciousness. We are the ones who suffer when we do that. We carry them when we worry about them, are concerned about them instead of releasing them to life, to love, to Truth. This means that we get busy filling our own moments with the highest of our Self.

The Truth sets us free so that we can soar in our own livingness. But in trying to get, to acquire and to have, we are burdened by what it is that we are going after. They are meant to be in our lives as freedom, not possession.

As we are actively expressing success, love and health, we are automatically helping others. Our greatest gifts to others come from living fully, from Being our Total Self. We then send off waves of energy that inspires and blesses. Thus the only way we can really help others is to help them help themselves. We are role models to others. We help them grow and mature by growing and maturing ourselves.

I find that when someone comes to me for treatment, prayer, the Truth that I know is infinitely more creative when I forget all about the person and deal only with the Truth. In releasing them I am not concerned about the outcome. I do not feel a false sense of responsibility. In freeing them, there is no worry, concern or doubt. When I try to remember them or recall them into my thought, there is a tendency to also bring back what they have said about their problem, and this certainly does not bless them or help them.

Since our thought is universal, everywhere present, and since the person who comes to us for help is already tuning in, then they are at one with those ideas that we are now knowing and living.

At all times you and I have a purpose. There is always something within us that needs to be given out and expressed in the here and now. We can only discover that purpose, that reason for being in the Eternal NOW, when we are living independently of person, situation, and thing as being cause. When we express love we are not involved with the person or the problem. We are simply giving, sharing and revealing. Love never makes demands and never expects returns, even though it always receives the rewards.

The expression of success is simply an outpouring of the fullness of the inner Self. God does not collect or acquire, even though It does become form. God is never involved with someone's problem because It is that which does not know what a problem is. It is the activity of sending out to this present moment whatever needs to be given in an uplifting and creative way.

We all have something to give to this moment. We cannot know what it is for each other. This must come from within our own Self. It is revealed to us what to give when we acknowledge the completeness and perfection that God already is as each of us.

Whatever we are obsessed with getting we do not have. We will never have it as long as we think about it in that way. It is the law of life that we only have what we give. We only have what we are now giving. There cannot be a continuous outpouring of love and joy when we are carrying things and people in our use of thought and are trying to mentally coerce something to happen for what we feel is right for them. You and I have no right to determine what is right for others and how they should live their lives.

We are universal. Our consciousness must be free and clear of the debris of yesterday. If we are to be effective in living life fully and joyously, we must release the problem and live the answer.

Our conscious use of thought is for the purpose of touching the True Self, the awareness of Who and What we really are. It is for the purpose of permitting that which already IS to be revealed through us, not to make something happen. Our positive use of thought is for the purpose of being able to give to the present moment only that which God is. However, when we are trying to get, when we are trying to add to our Self, we are never free to live. It is living that brings into our lives all that is for our highest good. We are always a prisoner of what we are trying to get, and what we are trying to get is really a denial that we are already complete.

We can only be effective in experiencing success when we are living the Truth. Being controlled by wish to have happen makes us ineffective. It is a divine unconcern about what is going to happen that permits us to live life fully in the now.

When we are at one with ideas of success we can release the individual, the situation, the thing. BEING then becomes our goal. Living becomes our purpose rather than the amassing of fortunes—although this can happen as a result of Being. The things we are trying to get happen when we stop trying to get and begin living the qualities that automatically bring them to us.

Each and every moment has its own demands. Not upon what someone else is doing, but upon what we ourselves are doing. There is always That within us that knows all that needs to be known, because Mind is Universal. What is known and expressed by us automatically draws to us whoever and whatever corresponds. Our Self-awareness and Self-expression draws out of Infinite Mind those ideas, those Truths, that are right for our challenges.

Mind gives to us an idea to know which is exactly right

for the present moment, blessing not only ourselves but those who come to our thought. However, we cannot receive that powerful and healing idea when we are hanging on to the person in our thought. The person becomes a shadow that gets in the way of creative Mind action. Mind is always where we are and we can make any claim upon It. Mind always responds. Mind gives to us thoughts, ideas, Truths, not things. Those ideas act upon Mind and Mind creates the form. What is necessary, however, is an IDEA. The things are automatic.

Where we live and work there are people. They are all seen through our own consciousness. If we believe them to be insipid, dishonest, callous or wasteful, that is judgment, and we are creating and experience of this for ourselves. We are seeing through our Self. Others can only be themselves, whatever that may be. Since we always find what we are looking for, why look through shadows when we can look through love? We must release the people in our lives to their own uniqueness and refrain from trying to change them to conform to our shadows.

We must free the people in our world as being problems so that we can live our own uniqueness and thus bless all that is in our own individual world. We stand at the center of our every experience and so we cannot look to our good or bad from anyone. There is neither good nor bad. There is only Self. Everything is created out of our Self. The forms "out there" are but shadows of the mind. Reality is within our own consciousness. All who are in our experience are here for us to know the Truth, nothing else.

Each person in our lives represents an idea, an aspect of our own identity. We experience that aspect or that idea with these people. We are really dealing, then, with something within our own Self. Because of the law of attraction people will always be in our life, but they are a response to what is going on within our consciousness. Since we are universal, then Mind brings to us whoever represents our Self.

When we seem to be arguing with someone else, we are really having a confrontation with our own Self—our own insecurity, self-rejection or our inner fears. When we seem to be hating someone, it is really an aspect of our own Self. When we seem to be loving someone, it is really an aspect of our own Self. Otherwise we would not be involved. When ours is the consciousness and expression of love, then there will be the people of love in our experience. The love that we ourselves are expressing is the power. The people of love who respond to our expressions of love are automatic.

You may say, "I simply cannot accept the idea that when I start to work in a new office that all of the people are there because of me and are suddenly going to change their behavior to fit me." That is not what I am saying. When we enter into any building, any office, we are seeing, hearing and interpreting through our own consciousness, through our own Self. Those people will continue to be themselves, but we are still seeing each and every one through our own past experience, through our now state of mind.. All of these people now become the people of our own Self, the people of our own interpretations. When we see them as being loving, beautiful, joyous and wonderful, that is what we experience. They are not the power. They are illusions or shadows of our mind.

Years ago when I first became a practitioner in the Science of Mind I used to keep a notebook that had in it the names of the people for whom I was treating. Next to the names I wrote their problem so that I would know what to treat for. At that point I encouraged treatment by the week or month. I soon began to realize what I was really doing. Each time that I looked at the name and the problem I was resurrecting the problem and had to once more treat to be free of it. Every time that I remembered the person it was in terms of his or her problem. However, it is the knowing of the Truth that sets us free, not in the knowing of the problem or of remembering people.

I began then to think only in terms of Truth and I then automatically forgot the person and his or her problem. It was then that the healings really began to take place. If the person came to mind once more, it was for me to consciously know the Truth, rather than the problem.

Many people tell me that they want me to remember them, if it comes to a choice, and to forget about the Truth. But it is the knowing of the Truth that helps them, not my remembering their names, their personalities and their challenges. My recalling their problems through visual images in my mind does not do them any good because the Reality is the Truth and Truth is above and beyond the problem. The images, the problems, the illusions to which they are giving their attention are but shadows of the mind.

When we pray for the person we are remembering the problem. When we identify the Truth we are freed by that Truth and it has nothing to do with person, situation or thing. the Truth that we ourselves know and live blesses not only our own Self and the person who requested treatment, but every single person we know because they are all within our consciousness and our consciousness is everywhere present at all times.

We must be in the world but not of it. This means that we all have work to do. We must be about the Father's business, the business of revealing the greatness of our Self. We must be in the world so that we can be an example of living that Truth. We must remember that the world is a reaction to our action—it is a shadow of the mind. The world is to us what we are to ourselves.

I do not help either myself or you if I go back into yesterday and remember what I think you did and said. What you did and said yesterday was, in my own experience, what I interpreted you to be doing and saying. Whatever you did and said is not really important. I am controlled by my interpretations. You have your own interpretation and I have mine. My experience is created out of what I believe I see and hear, and yours is created out of your interpretation of what you see and hear. If I am filled with envy or anxiety, then I have work to do on my own Self so that my interpretation is now in harmony with the Truth of Being—that God is everywhere present, uniquely expressed. I must make no judgment upon you and I must make no judgment upon my own Self.

We can only help each other by unifying with great ideas rather than small ones. We must let go of the illusion, the shadows, and consciously accept the Truth that we are already complete. Yes, we all have a long way to go in life, but it is a journey into Self-awareness rather than Self-improvement. When we accept that we are created in the image and likeness of God, we begin to act as though it is so.

In living this Truth, we must let go of the problem, let go of the outer and be fully at one with the Truth of our Being so that we can see clearly the greatness of the people in our lives.

The level of consciousness that I am is Universal, and WHOEVER tunes in is blessed. We do not have to send it out to a particular person. That is the job of Mind. We must simply KNOW and LIVE the Truth. We are then that Center beaming out the signals of that which we know. We let go of the shadows and function with

Reality, which is within our own consciousness.

When we are reacting to what others are doing and saying, we take ourselves out of the Universal Now and are putting ourselves into yesterday, into the memory of our interpretation of that which was. Our reaction to yesterday's interpretation is our now experience.

However, we are not here to react. We are here to act. When there is action going on there is no reaction and when there is no reaction there is freedom. Our reactions are always to shadows, not to reality. The reactions of others are really to something within their own consciousness. Yet the Truth is all powerful and the Truth that we know finds a way to bring back to us that which we are sending out.

When we release others and are giving our full attention to living the highest of ourselves, we are not excluding love. Love is the giving of the highest of our Self. It has no object. We are only free to love others when we are involved with love and not people. We experience love when we express love regardless of where we are or what we are doing. The expression of love causes Mind to attract into our life all that corresponds with the expression. We are here to help others by helping them to help themselves.

So often love is mistaken for pity or sympathy. It is neither. We are here to help others awaken to their great potential and powers within their Being, but we cannot do this by simply giving them handouts. Whenever we identify a person with an idea of limitation, we have not only taken that idea of limitation into our own consciousness, but we have directed into Mind that idea for others and we do not help them at all. We cannot help others by dealing with their problem, by trying to solve it for them, by talking about it as if there were something to be overcome.

Every time that we talk about our problems we are maintaining it in our experience. Our point of attention must always become form. That is the law. When we are involved with the problem of others we are making it our own. We are saying that this problem is a reality and must be overcome in some way. To be free of the problem we must transcend it and actively be at one with the Truth. It is just as exciting to be involved with Truth as it is to be involved with the problem.

It is the person with the undeveloped spiritual consciousness who loves to sit around with others and talk about their own problems, and the problems of others. These are the gossips of the world. However, when we are consciously acknowledging the wholeness of our True Self, there are great ideas to expound. We are universal, and all that we say and do is an influence upon the world. We must all realize that why we are here is not to live unto ourselves but to let greatness live through us.

We help others arrive at Self-awareness by our recognizing always the sufficiency and completeness that each and every one truly IS. There can be no exceptions. If God is all there is, and this we must accept, then there are no exceptions.

It is the function of those who are Self-aware—which is each of us—to KNOW and to LIVE the Truth. It is our function to release Truth into active expression. When we have done this, we have fulfilled our purpose—To KNOW the Truth, to LIVE the Truth and to RELEASE it. Releasing it means letting go of the results, letting go of how it is to be manifested in either our own experience or that of others. Truth is not something that we memorize and repeat over and over again. It is something that we live. We must always be receptive to larger ideas. We must be open to that inner voice of the Total Self that gives through us ideas of unfoldment, ideas of greater and greater insight.

The purpose of treatment, of meditation, affirmations, and prayer is to bring us to a point of living, of doing, of giving. So often in hanging on to yesterday's affirmation, to yesterday's treatment, we are getting in the way of today's new idea, in the way of today's purpose, in the way of new NOW thought. It is the NOW that must be our concern, our point of attention. Since today is all there is, we must be at one with today's purpose, today's work.

We all have something creative to give to the present moment. What is it? There is that within each of us that knows for our own individual Self. There is That within me that knows for me. There is that within you that knows for you. Whatever it is, it is a giving and sharing purpose. It can only come through the active recognition of Who and What we really are. When we have a sense of separation, we always try to get. We always try to add to our Self.

I believe that we must change the usual approach to the Science of Mind and go in the opposite direction. Too many of us are using it for the purpose of getting something rather than revealing or giving something. The glorious thing to realize is that automatically Mind brings back to us what we are sending out, as long as our motivation is that of giving, not getting.

We must use our thought to be aware of the power of God that we already are so that we can be aware of the power of God that EVERY person potentially is. This is our gift to whoever is in our experience.

There is the purpose of this present moment. Only the infinite Intelligence within our own Self can reveal what it is. Every once in a while someone will ask me, "Are you thinking of me? Are you remembering my need?" I usually say, "Of course," and let it go at that because otherwise their feelings might be hurt. However, I cannot help anyone by remembering their problem, by thinking of them as being limited in any way. If I acknowledge that God is all there is, then I must be aware of that wholeness that already is, not their problem.

When someone comes to us it is for the purpose of being in tune with the completeness of the NOW, not the problems of yesterday. Love is that which recognizes sufficiency NOW, regardless of who is in our Consciousness. Love is that which looks through the Consciousness of Truth and sees that Truth is the reality of ALL.

To get back to Principle, if God is all there is, and this we must actively accept if we are to be free, then there is no problem. If God is all there is, then all that God is—IS.

We only have problems when we are not minding our own business, when we are living in either yesterday or tomorrow. We have a problem when we try to get something rather than to express or give something. Since God is all there is, then the problem did not exist yesterday, it does not exist today and it will not exist tomorrow because there never was any problem. If the problem is merely a shadow of the mind, and it is, it is illogical to try to overcome it day after day.

When someone comes into our thought, they are there for us to know ideas of wholeness and perfection, not to remember their problem. It is useless to try to overcome a shadow, an illusion. You may say, "That is all very easy for you to say because you are not the one who is suffering. I'm the one who's got the pain. I'm the one who has been given the verdict." But the pain is there, the verdict is there, because you have been trying to get something or overcome something.

When we get all caught up in the problem we are using our thought to separate our Self from Who and What we really are. We are again dealing with a shadow of the Mind. The problem is only very real to us because we choose to believe in it. What we are dealing with is a belief, an illusion and there is no reality in illusion.

I know someone who every time she hears of a friend or loved one suffering some sort of physical ailment takes on the symptoms of that ailment and suffers accordingly. This sympathy is a shadow of the Mind and she experiences it. When I show her what she has been doing and we actively acknoweledge the perfection of her Self, the symptoms instantly go away.

GOD IS ALL THERE IS. That is the approach that we must take. Otherwise we are going to be involved with shadows....Shadows of the Mind.

I have often received phone calls from various "students" who have said, "I wrote you a letter yesterday asking you to treat for me. When you get the letter just ignore it because I have already been healed." How can this happen? Did they heal themselves? Or did they tune into an idea, into a level of Consciousness, a choice, that I represent to them? By taking some kind of action to be free did Mind take care of the details? It is all the same thing. I am Universal. You are Universal. There is One Mind. What I am knowing where I am is everywhere present and all who tune in are blessed.

Conversely, whoever is sympathetic to the problems of others is tuning in to that level of thought and they must reap the consequences themselves.

When we are in a negative state of mind, when we are fearful or anxious or depressed, no one would turn to us for help except those who are in tune with that level of Consciousness. The law of attraction is forever in action. If ours are to be the people of love, we must be the person of love first of all. If our experience is to be filled with the forms of abundance, beauty, and joy, then we must be abundance, beauty and joy in action. We only know what we are NOW expressing.

Wallowing in self-pity can only attract to that level of Consciousness pitiful experiences and pitiful people. We are universal and Mind only attracts to us those who are on our wave length. Mind goes to great lengths to bring to us those who represent our Self. The more that we are Self-aware, aware of all that God is by means of us, the more Mind draws to us those who can be helped or inspired by that level of Consciousness that we are now living.

When we believe in ourselves, respect ourselves, even then there is no problem. Even then there is nothing to overcome because our Self-love, Self-esteem, is all that we need. It is the answer to everything. Our consciousness of Love does not permit any problem to exist in our life. We can only hear and see that which is within our Consciousness.

When someone comes to us and says, "Look, I've got this great problem and I desperately need your help," we are against Principle when we say, "Tell me all about it." They may want to talk and get something off their chest, but if we encourage them to tell us all of the gory details about everything that is wrong in their experience, we are going to get caught up in a belief that there is indeed something to be corrected of a serious nature. The more serious we see it to be, the more difficult it is to be free of it.

Our awareness of the Presence is absolutely vital. Our awareness of the sufficiency of the other is necessary. If we believe that God is all there is, even as the person is telling us his or her story, in our thought there is still no problem. The other person may believe that there is a problem, but what has that got to do with us or with Truth? NOTHING! It is certainly an opportunity to know the Truth, and what we must do. We must not be swept away with their interpretation.

There are times that I let people talk because it saves me from having to argue with them. It saves me from having to detach myself. It saves me from having to say that they are wrong. I am always dealing with my own Consciousness, my own use of thought, not theirs. There is nothing to argue about. There is only something to KNOW. There must be an active recognition on my part that GOD IS ALL THERE IS.

This moment, in the here and now, is the only moment there is. This moment, which is where God resides, is all there is. If we live this present moment as love, as the Presence of God, then we live in peace and all who turn to us receive the peace that we are now express-ing. We cannot live that peace if we are trying to get something, if we are filled with a great need for something, if we are fighting someone, or if we are try-ing to overcome a shadow in the mind that has no basis in reality.

Peace is the acknowledgement of One Power. It is a result of an absence of conflict. There is conflict when we believe that there are two rather than one. There is no conflict when we are no longer trying to do something about someone else.

When we release the people in our lives as to what they are doing and how they are doing it, and concern ourselves instead with living fully in the present moment, giving the highest of our Self to all that we do, there is peace. When we make our claim upon Mind for what we need to know, so that we can give to the pres-ent moment for the highest good of all, there is no con-flict. There is simply the expression of our Total Self.

In the experience of peace we make no claim upon anyone. We do not demand anything of anyone. Thus there is peace. There is always conflict when we seek agreement from others. Nothing can touch us except that which we ourselves are expressing. If we are expressing love, no one can hurt us or take away our good. It is only when we make a demand upon someone, even by means of treatment, that there is conflict within our consciousness and we then have a problem.

Whoever reaches out to us, whether in person or in mind, must receive what we are, what we are giving. Whoever responds to us must receive from our Beingness, of that which we are thinking, feeling and giving. The moment they reach out to us they instantly receive all that we are now expressing, even if they reach out by means of thought, by means of the acknowledgement of our presence. There is no delay for we are Universal.

Mind is everywhere present and there is but One Mind. In universality, we are not dealing with books, letters, conversation, or body. We are dealing with Universal Being. The moment that anyone reaches out in consciousness, they receive out of Mind whatever it is they need to know to go through a challenge for Mind always responds to the claim that is made upon it.

We have a definite responsibility, you and I, in knowing that we are here to help and to bless others, in knowing that we are universal. In this realization, we have the opportunity and the responsibility to be living the Truth at all times. This is not a burden. It is truly a joy, for this blesses our Self always. Not only are we blessing others by being the example, but we ourselves are blessed by the Truth that we know and live. We automatically help others by helping ourselves, by living the Truth. All that we have to give at any time is our Self. We must be prepared by creating a consciousness of Truth, of Love.

When we are knowing the Truth, however, we must not outline how that Truth is to become form, either for ourselves or for others. If, in knowing the Truth for others, we mentally try to get them to behave in the way that we want them to behave, we are going to try to correct them in some way. This only causes conflict. It is mental manipulation. Instead, we must release others. In my own appraoch I do not even mention a name. I simply know and live the Truth, and however that Truth is manifested through others is none of my business. It must come forth uniquely as them, not me.

Loving our neighbor as our Self is an important principle because our neighbor is our Self. What we know for him we know for our Self. When we are told to pray for our enemies, this again is only practical because any enemies that we have are within our own consciousness.

It is important that our consciousness be free and clear of any anger or fear. We cannot afford to carry any grudges or resentment within our Self because, not only is our own Self affected, but we are not free to help others when our consciousness is distorted with these shadows of the mind. We are universal and we are here to help others by knowing and living the Truth. We help others by radiating love.

We are really here to give out only that which is worthwhile, that which blesses, inspires and sustains. Doing this instantly touches every area of our own lives, even though the motivation is to help others.

When we awaken in the morning we should not have one single problem on our mind. If we do, it means that we did not do our work as the challenge came along. *It means that we are giving our attention to effect rather than to cause!*

There should be no problem people in our consciousness. If we are eternally acknowledging that God is the only power, there are no problem people with whom to contend.

You may say that if you don't take care of all of the mistreated animals in the world, who will? You may certainly be the instrument through which dogs and cats find new homes or are taken care of physically and loved, but if you are knowning the Truth that God is everywhere present, you will not see it as a problem. You will play your part and you will be knowing the Truth that touches every dog or cat that comes into your experience.

When we actively acknowledge that *God is all there is,* we are filled with a sense of power, a feeling of authority. We know that God is in charge and that there is nothing to fear. We can then go forth with the certainty that we always know what to do as it needs to be done. We can go into the day knowing that it is a day of adventure and creative work and that God is giving through us greatly and inspiringly. We are then not concerned with what is going to happen because we know that only God can happen.

Consciousness must become form. When we are declaring into the law of Mind that God is all there is, then whatever comes to our attention is interpreted correctly and we are free to release and not carry it around with us.

We may not know why someone has come to us in thought. But our being aware that we know all that we need to know as we need to know it causes Mind to reveal the purpose of the moment. It may not reveal the person's problem, but we are told from within that Truth it is that we must know. That Truth must instantly bless whoever it is that comes to our thought. Then we have done what we are supposed to do and we do not have to try to remember them later, when it might be too late.

You and I have a responsiblity to the Universe to reveal

the Presence of God. We are not here to live just for ourselves or just for our families. We are universal. What we are knowing and living and feeling and doing right now is affecting everything in our consciousness.

If we are not actually inside of our home but are elsewhere, our home still resides within our consciousness and is affected by this consciousness, which is everywhere present. What we know is in subconscious mind, which is universal. We are not our body. We have a body and that body lives within our consciousness. Our body, our home, our pets, our clothes (even the ones in our closets) are being affected by what we are being right now. We owe it to the Universe to be our God Self in action right now. We cannot live unto our Self. Mind is everywhere present and there is but one Mind.

We owe it to the people in our world to be our own unique Self, to live out of our sufficiency, to discover the greatness that is within so that we can then share. We must give to the people in our world the Truth that they desire and deserve by giving them their freedom to be and by our living the Truth to the best of our ability always.

Instead of deciding how others should behave and what they should express, we must release them and be at one with the universal power of our Self-awareness and our Self-expression. The people in our lives deserve the very best because they are individualizations of God. But so are we...and the best is ours to give.

CHAPTER VII

Success
is
Individual

Whatever we have in the way of success in our life, we demonstrated it individually and we are individually expressing it. No one can really do it for us. We ourselves are the ones who are always directing Mind. We are the ones who are thinking, doing, and expressing our own individualization of Life. No one can live for us. Each one of us is directing Mind in our own way and Mind is creating everything that corresponds. To lean upon anyone else in any way except in an interconnecting manner is restricting our own doing, our own use of those inner resources that are to be found within us all.

If we try to get someone to breathe for us, we will not last very long. It is our own breathing that keeps the body alive. If we try to get someone else to eat for us, we would soon starve to death. It is what we ourselves eat that counts. If we try to get someone else to do our thinking for us, we would soon be at their mercy, never being able to make a move if they are not there. Should they go out of our life, we would have to find someone else to tell us what to do. We would then never know the excitement and freedom of living out of our own Self.

Those who look outside of their Self for their answers

are always afraid to be alone, and they desperately attach themselves to others and hang on for dear life. They are letting shadows of the mind tell them how to live.

There is a family I know with Mom and Dad, daughter and son. The daughter had to play an active part in the family experience because girls are expected to help with the housework, the functions of everyday family life. The son, being a boy, was not expected to do anything, and so he was catered to and got out of any kind of work or responsibility at home. They eventually grew up and are now young adults.

The daughter went to college and, after graduation, found a job. After a while she decided to get her own apartment and be on her own. She now has her own car, a beautiful wardrobe, soon bought a condominium and is making her own life.

The son, however, didn't like to study so he dropped out of school. He arrived at the age where he needed his own car, but he didn't have any money for one so his folks bought him one. He tried getting a job, but he discovered that he did not like to work, that he couldn't be bothered with the hours of a regular schedule. So he quit. He began having one accident after another with his car and could not afford to have it repaired. Now Mom and Dad find that they have a monster on their hands. They wish that he would get his own apartment, but he can't even afford to stay at home.

The parents have, in effect, crippled thier son by not teaching him to live out of his own Self, to think for himself or to direct Mind by his own active expression of sufficiency.

We never help others by doing their work. We never help others by doing their thinking for them. Life is always an individual experience. When we learn to express our Self in ways of strength and greatness, the more we are a blessing to the people in our life.

Very little progress can be made in life until we really know Who and What we are. We cannot really proceed into success unless we know the part that God must play in our life. Not God as a power outside of our Self, but God, that Presence, that reality of our own Being. Until we are actively Self-aware, and actively living as the AUTHORITY in our every moment can we really go somewhere.

Even in the Science of Mind many people would prefer that God be left out of it. They would like to take the "I" and claim it as being their own, as their name, as their separate unit. We can certainly direct Mind at the level of ego, of separation, but ego runs out. Ego is not dealing with an infinite, limitless Power. It is a separation of that Power. Using the teaching at the level of ego demands that we look to others to help us, rather than drawing upon something from within. It demands that we blame others when things go wrong. It sees success as being something that we get rather than something that we express.

Some people say that God is really ego because without it we would not demand our rights, our share of the pie. God, however, is simply the fullness within our Self that demands to be expressed, that demands that we stand up and assert ourselves. This is born out of completeness, not incompleteness.

Self-awareness is a way of life, not something that we receive. Living the Presence frees us from the shadows of the mind that are created out of our dependency. We must make every demand upon our own inner Self rather than upon others. We must let the law of our Being take care of the details while we individualize success, love, health, and prosperity.

Someone was given a medical verdict that terrified her.

She called me in an effort to get me to put all of my experience and know how to work to overcome this physical manifestation. She asked me if she should also treat, pray. This revealed that she had no idea that health is an individual experience. I can treat, I can know the Truth, but unless each of us is tuning in and letting that Truth be alive within our own consciousness, then I am the only one blessed by the Truth because I am the one who is individually knowing it and living it.

If you are tuning in, the healing may be temporary because it is not your way of life, it is not your individual knowing, living and doing that is directing Mind in your own experience. This is very much a "do it yourself" teaching. My purpose as a teacher is to get others to arrive at the point where they are doing it for themselves.

So many people say that they understand all of the principles intellectually, but that does not seem to change their life. Of course it wouldn't. It couldn't. It is only what we ourselves are individually expressing that works. Self-awareness is the beginning, but it must move into Self-expression as well. No one else can do this for us. Success is fabulous and very worthwhile, but it is something that we give, not what we get. Success is what we are individually expressing, and Mind accepts this expression and creates the forms thereof.

Anything that takes us away from expressing our self-sufficiency we should avoid. When we choose to express our self-sufficiency and do it, we will not demonstrate people who want to take care of us, pamper us, control us and manipulate us. If this is the kind of people we have in our lives, we have chosen them very carefully. We always have in our lives the people of our Self. If we have controlling people in our lives, we are the ones who are going to suffer in the long run.

In the middle of the night the phone rings. I answer

and it is someone telling me of a life and death emergency. I assure the person that I am already knowing the Truth, I assure him or her of my love and tell the individual that I am already knowing the Truth. I release him or her to whatever needs to be done while I relax in the knowingness that God is all there is.

If I am fooled into believing that it is an emergency, that there is some great problem to overcome, I would not be able to help anyone.

Everytime someone comes to us for help there is the temptation to try to help. There is the temptation to believe that there really is a problem. The people in our lives can be very persuasive. They are filled with a belief that is causing them to fall apart. But they are being controlled by a shadow of the mind. A belief is using them. We must not be tempted into accepting their belief and make it ours. They are having their lesson to learn, their challenge, their opportunity to become aware of the great power within their own Self.

If there is only one Power, and there is, and that Power is God, and It is, then there is nothing to overcome. There is only God. There is certainly something to do because God is an action. There is something to KNOW and something to DO. Knowing includes action.

The following morning after the phone call I received another call from the same person telling me that there was an instantaneous healing. I could not even be tempted into believing that there was a healing because if God is all there is, there was nothing to be healed. Only something to be KNOWN. Only something of which to be aware.

You may say, "Are you trying to tell me that this person was not sick? That he was only fooling?" I am not saying that at all. The person who was experiencing the physical pain and the person who was witnessing it were both seeing something happen as pain. Their belief in the effect caused them to maintain it. In calling me they chose to be at one with a perfect cause. My non-acceptance of the problem and my active acceptance of God as being EVERYWHERE present permitted their belief to be changed. Body always corresponds to belief.

Every challenge that comes to us is merely a divine opportunity to know the Truth. And the Truth is that God is ALL THERE IS.

The law of attraction is not necessarily going to attract to us only those who believe the same way we do. It is not going to attract to us only those who are exactly like us. It attracts to us those who help us move forward, who bring us challenges, who help us know the Truth in a greater way. Our knowing the Truth is not necessarily going to cause the cost of living to go down. Our knowing the Truth, however, permits us to have all that represents our Self, regardless of the cost. Do not be tempted by what the news media says. Do not be tempted by what the prices say on the items you would like to have. These are all shadows of the mind. If you believe what the world says is so, then you must experience that belief. However, if we accept that God is all there is, then that is the answer for every challenge that comes along, no matter what that challenge is.

Success is still an individual experience and this means that the world has nothing to do with it. We must stop listening to the world and begin listening to the voice of our God-Self. God already IS. We are created in the image and likeness of God, therefore our completeness already IS. Nothing can take it away. It IS and always shall be. But if we are tempted to believe the voices of the world, the shadows of the mind, then God is still where we are, but we are believing something else. We always experience our belief.

Our temptations always seem to come to us via some

person. And too many of us believe in the power of people to be cause to our experience. That tempation may also appear to us as something that we label good. We may receive a gift of a large sum of money. We call that good, when all it is is money. It is our consciousness drawing to us that which represents our Self. In rejoicing in the money we are putting the power of belief in money. Or, let us say, we are putting our belief in the power of money. But there is no power in money. Money cannot think. It cannot decide. It is consciousness that does this.

We must not be tempted into believing anything that comes to us as being a reality. It is simply a reflection of our Self. It may be very solid and physically substantial, but it is still a result, and not a cause. We still interpret it in terms of our own Self. When we are Self-aware and are individualizing success, then all that comes to us is but an opportunity to express success in some way. Every situation is an opportunity to know that there is a Presence guiding and directing our way in the giving of Truth in a unique and expanding way. There is that within us that is equal to any and every challenge. God already IS.

Close friends and family so often come to us and tell us all of the lurid details of what is going on in their life. We feel very close to them and we listen. We offer sympathy, advice, money and whatever else we can think of in the way of help. But all of this indicates that we have accepted the problem as being a reality. In this way of thought we are taken away from their sufficiency, from theirs. We see them as being inadequate, which does not help them at all.

Even our loved ones must arrive at the point where they themselves are individualizing success, love, Truth, God. We must not be tempted into doing their thinking for them and making their choices for them. We must not be tempted into doing their work for them. When their individual consciousness draws into their life what the world calls good, we must rejoice with them, but all the while know that it is still consciousness becoming form.

It is our labeling something as being good or bad that causes us to believe in the power of that form. There is neither good nor bad. There is only consciousness individualizing. It becomes visible. This visibleness tells us what is within our consciousness. But even then we must not be tempted to judge our Self. God never sits in judgment upon Itself. It just goes about the business of giving of Itself fully to each and every moment. That is exactly what we are meant to do because we are God's means to be. This giving cannot take place when we are fooled into believing that there is power in form.

As long as we are individualizing success we are pouring out into expression the infiniteness of our God-being. The forms must be there because consciousness always becomes form. Mind cannot say no.

We must be a blessing to the world, to our loved ones, by looking beyond all that they say and do and know that God is everywhere present as ALL. Regardless.

Be ye not tempted by the beliefs of the world, these shadows of the mind. The reality is God, life, love.

Many people who claim to be seeking the Truth are unwilling to let go of that which gets in the way of living the Truth. Their priorities seem to be what they can get rather than the Truth or living the Presence of God. Every goal that we set for ourselves restricts our degree of living the Truth. Each and every goal limits us to that goal. We have to have direction always, purpose, but when those goals are things rather than living, we are controlled by the goals and our living may be in great jeopardy.

For the most part, goals are for the purpose of getting

rather than of living. We may have a goal to demonstrate our own home, or a new and bigger house. We may have a goal of demonstrating a million dollars, of marrying a millionaire, of demonstrating a significant other. But all of these goals have their built in price to pay. Yes, the goal can be attained. We can use the science of mind to attain these goals. But in what we seek always brings with it a price to pay. If there are all kinds of strings attached, the goal is not going to be really fulfilling.

If you are willing to pay the price, go ahead. One may say that the price to pay is the building of consciousness, which, of course, is true. But the goal of building consciousness or of living the Presence is really PURPOSE. What I mean by goals is the acquiring or attaining of something or someone. The goal of landing a certain person as our mate must automatically exclude our right to be our own Self, for in order to get and hold that person we may have to let him or her call the shots. We may have to give up the uniqueness that we really are so that they can maintain their uniqueness.

The purpose of living the Presence or of living out of the Whole Self results in giving, sharing, revealing, BEING. The goal of getting that house puts full attention upon how we can get it, who we can use, how it is to come to us. The goal itself has within itself the means to accomplish its own ends, just as within every idea is the Intelligence of the Universe that knows how to fulfill that idea. There is a great difference between letting a goal tell us what we must do and letting the law of the Self take care of the details in every area of our life.

The goal may cause us to do unscrupulous things. It may cause us to cheat or to steal. It may cause us to step all over someone and try to take away their good just so that we can get ours. It may cause us to compete. It may cause us, in the vernacular, to "sell our Soul." In the attaining of any goal we have to outwit, to outrun.

We have to try to get God to be on our side rather than on the side of others.

PURPOSE, on the other hand, lets go of all of that and it maintains its own integrity. PURPOSE permits us to live out of our God-Self. It causes us to give the highest of our Self at all times to whatever we are doing in every moment. The goal excludes everything that stands in the way of that goal. But what it may exclude, such as love, joy, health, and freedom, are more important than the goal itself.

We have all seen examples of those who are totally dedicated to the achieving of their goals, no matter what, and in order to do so they have had to release loving relationships. They have sacrificed their morality, their health, their peace of mind, just to get where they wanted to be.

PURPOSE excludes all that does not correspond with the expression of Itself, but since it is filled with recognition of the inner Presence, it is expressed individually, with authority, love, joy and freedom. Since consciousness must always become form, then the body, the opportunities, the things, must automatically be there, but now they are in harmony with integrity. They merely help us to live in a greater and freer way. PURPOSE helps us experience balance. The goal takes us out of balance and accentuates only the goal.

Are our priorities to be our Self in action, to live fully and completely in every area of our life, or are they the acquiring of the house or the person? The house is not worth it if we are slave to the house. The person is not worth it if we are not free to grow and to discover and use our potential.

There are those who are living out of their inner Self and because Mind always creates form, they are living in beautiful and gracious homes. They have affluence and all that is necessary to live beautifully. They may be seen to be a part of the "goal seekers" but they are totally free in their environment.

Living the Presence of God does not mean that we take a vow of poverty or chastity and live in a very small way. We cannot deny Consciousness and what it produces. Money is wonderful when it's merely a reflection of the prosperity that we live, which is living the Presence. We cannot live the Presence without having a good deal of money. In the living of the Presence the priority is to express God. The money and homes and beauty are simply forms that represent Completeness.

When we have a goal of getting, of demonstrating some thing, Mind guides and directs our way to the acquiring of that goal. Mind always reveals what we need to know in order to fulfill either our purpose or our goals. But the goals of getting make us give up balance in our lives. The goals of getting make us do whatever those goals tell us to do so that we may acquire them.

In living success, success reveals all that we need to know in order to reveal our Total Self at all times. This Presence directs Mind and it touches every area of our lives, and puts all into balance. there is no need to escape into alcohol, drugs, food. There is no need to run away.

For the minister, the purpose is to teach principle, to help others awaken to their sufficiency. The larger church building then happens. But if the building is the goal, then the minister has to squeeze the congregation out of whatever money they have in order to get that new structure built. The teaching is then sacrificed. For hundreds of years the teachings of Jesus were sacrificed so that the church could have total power. But...Power is always individual and each one of us is meant to use it.

When our priority is to fulfill our potential, we live in the eternal now and we always have work to do. The purpose is to always reveal our God-nature, and this can only bless all on our pathway. The things that come to us because of the law of attraction, cannot be denied. Since there is nothing outside of our consciousness in our life, then our consciousness is where the power is. It is building, attaining and maintaining our God-Consciousness that should be the great purpose of our life. To believe that someone in our life is causing our problems is a failure on our part to realize that there is nothing outside of Consciousness.

To believe that someone is taking away our good or withholding it is to be ignorant of the law of our Being. Each of us must individualize all that we desire to experience. We only have what we express.

Humility is one aspect of life that most of us in the Living of the Presence of God teachings are accused of not having. We seem to be living life so zestfully, dynamically, seemingly aggressively, that those who are not doing the same thing are either envious or angry. Humility has nothing to do with being meek, mild and quiet. Humility is the realization that we are only complete through living the Presence. Humility is the realization that we of our own selves can do nothing and that we are God's means to live. To believe that we are complete because of what we have collected at the level of things or education is being very materialistic. Humility is letting go of the outer and living out of the inner kingdom of Truth, Life, God.

God cannot live in a small, constricted or insignificant way. God, being Self-complete, can only express Itself with joy, love, zest and enthusiasm. We are dynamic when we are sure of our Self. We are sure of our Self when we are consciously tuning in to the Inner Presence and are permitting It to live in terms of Its greatness through all that we think, say and do.

Those who are insecure about themselves are always

judging others. They compare. They criticize others for doing what they themselves would really like to be doing. We are admonished not to ''hide our light''—and when we acknowledge that the light comes from the Inner Self, which is God, then that light must burn brightly.

It is really the shy individual who lives at the level of ego. He or she is shy because there has been separation in thought from the Source. We are shy because we compare, because we are looking for a reaction from the world. We are shy because we fear what others think, which is a form of getting. We are shy because we do not believe in our Self.

Humility, on the other hand, gives full and complete recognition to the Inner Presence and lets that Presence live through us in terms of Itself. Knowing and acknowledging actively that it is the Father within that doeth the. work puts the responsibility where it belongs—on God.

If we are acknowledging this Presence, if we are individualizing this Presence, then It is expressing Itself through the uniqueness that It is as each one of us, and It is doing whatever It is doing with power, and It is doing it greatly.

Ulcers are a result of not being humble, of trying to make something happen on our own. Ulcers are a result of trying to get. We may believe that we are non-aggressive, that no one could accuse us of trying to get. But, even if we are seeking the approval of others by doing what they want us to do, that is still trying to get. When we deny the expression of what we are really all about we can only experience some kind of eruption within the body.

Each of us has work to do. It is a work of greatness because it is the work of God, of Life. Since God is infinite, then we are individualizing Infiniteness. We must stop concerning ourselves about what that work must be. This inner Presence reveals what needs to be known and let Itself be expressed through all that we do.

Jesus is certainly an example of someone who expressed himself strongly. He taught principle. He was not the meek and mild individual that some movies portray. He taught principle through his active Self-expression. He is the symbol of God in action through each of us.

We help others by our own example of living the Truth. We direct the law of Mind by our own example. We are here to let the light shine with power, love, joy and a dynamic expression of life.

We may feel that this does not suit our own personality at all. We may define our own personality as being shy, quiet and very sweet. But when we identify with the idea of God "as me" and act as though it is so, then all that God is comes pouring forth through us and we do whatever we do with authority, sureness and limitless energy. In this way we are simply BEING—free of the concern of how we are going over.

It is not a matter of redoing our whole personality. Living the Presence of God, individualizing success, does not demand that we give up our uniqueness. It permits us to truly discover it since we are now free, daring to be, and are no longer concerned about getting.

Again, we must always remember that what we are expressing and the way that we are expressing it is the way that we are directing Mind. The treatment merely leads us to the expression. Humility is being involved with expression rather than with the reaction of the world. Humility is the recognition that there is the intelligence of God working through all of the people in our life and releasing them to their own answers, to their own inner uniqueness, whatever that may be.

Humility is acknowledging that our own answers do

not come from the world but from this inner Intelligence. Humility is the active letting go of outlining how our good is to come to us and releasing it all to the law of God, the law of the Total Self. We can be so organized as to the demonstration of our goals, the goals of getting what we want, that we take ourselves completely out of the health, wealth and success of today.

Success is not what we are going to get, but what we are now expressing. Success is not the money that is going to come to us or has already come to us, but what we are now expressing regardless of where we are. In Truth we are already complete. We are Self-complete only through our active indentification with that Presence that we call God.

As we release the accomplishments of yesterday and live out of this inner genius, this Presence, then new and greater aspects of the Total Self can come forth into expression. Then our work becomes important, no matter what we are doing. When we are expressing love, that action can only reflect the allness of God, because God is love.

Body is always formed by Mind out of Consciousness. Whatever is within that consciousness is what appears as body, as the forms in our life. We are so often trying to heal the body, when the body has no power. It is merely a way of thought become form. This is why we can never really effectively do anything about someone whom we feel is hurting us, or whom we see to be lacking in a variety of ways. We are seeing through our own consciousness and what we are fighting is a shadow of the mind, a concept, an idea that we are using.

Our demanding that others shape up is getting in the way of our experience of love. There are many people who are absolute fanatics about smokers, drinking, sugar, salt, organic foods, etc. They are fanantical about it for themselves and they demand the same of others. Even in this teaching they feel that if the law of attraction is always in action, why is it bringing into their lives people who smoke, drink, eat junk food and do everything that they themselves do not do. Yes, like attracts like. The law of attraction always brings into our lives those who represent ourselves.

If there is something within us that is so demanding upon others, the law is going to bring into our lives those who frustrate those demands. They represent our consciousness of battle. Fanaticism is really battle. It is something that is out of balance. It demands but one way. Our way. And it demands it of others. Since it is looking for a fight it will find one. Mind always cooperates. If we are to be free, to live creatively, we can make demands only upon our own Self. If we believe that power is in the cigarette, alcohol, food, etc., then all of these are controlling our experience as we actively avoid them, as we actively fight them.

Our consciousness of Truth may cause us to eat certain foods. Fine. But we are not the uniqueness of someone else. Their consciousness may cause them to eat other kinds of foods. These foods may or may not be right for them. Diet does not make consciousness. Smoking or not smoking does not make consciousness. It is not cause to anything. They are symptoms, not cause. The real body is Consciousness, and Consciousness is made up of Self-contemplation, Self-awareness. We can perfect body by exercise, eating certain kinds of foods, wearing the right clothes, using the right make-up, getting the right hair style, etc. and we can look the picture of beauty. If there is not something more, it is only a picture that is empty. If we are not radiating joy, enthusiasm, love and energy, the picture is a vacuum and it is really nothing.

It is the Consciousness of love, joy, vitality that is the

real body of God, of the Total Self. This inner Intelligence always directs our way in our use of things. When we are using our thought to activate the consciousness of God, our Total Self, then we are guided automatically in our use of food, things, etc.

We are so often bound by the concepts of yesterday, by traditions, and these shadows of the mind get in the way of something new coming through our Self-expression. Traditions are created as a means of feeling secure. They are, however, not security. We are only secure when we are expressing our God-Self in new and different ways, when we are revealing the specialness that we truly are.

When we are living in the now and are giving the highest of our Self to the opportunities and challenges at hand we are knowing security. When we are bound by traditions, which are merely concepts, we are letting these concepts get in the way. Fanatics are bound by form, by behavior, by yesterday. Their judgment of what should happen can very well get in the way of their demonstrating the ideal mate, the ideal job, the ideal opportunity.

Yes, by all means have integrity. But integrity is really living the Presence of God, being true in our own expression of life to the nature of God. Integrity does not demand that others stop thinking for themselves. It does not demand that others be exactly the way we want them to be. The integrity that we ourselves live does not permit others to lead us astray. It does permit us to live in freedom, while giving others the very same right.

So many of us seek to demonstrate the right mate, and when someone comes into our life who does not fit our exact demands, we then plan on changing them as soon as we walk up the aisle. But they won't be changed, they insist upon remaining themselves and so we are unhappy. It is our concept getting in the way. We are fighting a shadow of the mind.

Many people worship Jesus. But they all have a different concepts of Jesus, depending upon which movie they have seen, which paintings they have viewed, and what their own particular needs may be. Artists have different concepts. He sometimes looks like the typical concept of a Jewish Rabbi or a blond Viking. But it is the Christ that Jesus represents, and the Christ is not body. The Christ is the individual experience of living the Presence of God. It is the individual expression of that inner power that we call God.

Disease is the result of a false concept of Self, and of fighting the concepts of others, of trying to make them all conform to what we want. We are afraid of certain people because of the power that they represent to us. But we are fearing a shadow for they represent something within our own consciousness. The real body, then, is our own consciousness. We must fill that consciousness with Truth. We must individualize that Truth and release others to do their own thing. Mind then helps us to fulfill the Truth that we are expressing and we are always free of trying to get something or someone. All that is required in our life to live fully is automatically there for Consciousness must always become form.

We are a concept of Self. When we permit that concept to be free of the traditions of yesterday by consciously acknowledging the Godness of our Self, then we have no problems. Our Total Self, which already is, is already whole and complete. When we accept that completeness we do not have to add to our Self by accumulating more and more things. When we express our Self-acceptance, Mind creates the forms of that Self, and It also guides and directs our way into the opportunities that reflect that Self.

183

We cannot deny body. Body is. Consciousness must always become form. That is the law. In our world, since consciousness becomes form, since there are things and people, it is necessary to eat, to work, sleep, pay our income taxes, to clean the house, write letters, etc. In living the Presence we do not avoid all of these activities. We are involved with them as Self-expression and this is vastly different from being materialistically oriented. We are told to be in the world but not of it, and this is true. In our activities we must see them all as an opportunity to live the Truth, to live the Presence.

In the living of Truth, that Truth must evolve as person, situations and things. In living the Truth we may be guided to go to a doctor, we may be guided to eat certain foods, we may be guided to exercise, we may be guided to make a phone call. We are not here to avoid the world. So many people who first come into this teaching give up reading newspapers, watching television, going to movies or reading books other than those that are metaphysical because they do not want to be involved in negativity. But we cannot avoid our friends and relatives. We cannot avoid the world for Mind is always being directed by us to bring into our lives whoever and whatever represents our Self.

The temptation that we always have with us is the becoming involved with the world as cause. The world, however, is not cause—it is merely effect. It is always to us what we are to ourselves. Mind brings into our life the people and situations that help us to experience our Self. Also the things. It is when we believe that it is our own cleverness that takes us through challenges that we begin to have problems. It is then that we begin to be in the world as well as of it. The world is an outpicturing of our Consciousness. It is our Self become form or experience. However, we must remember that our reaction is always our experience.

All power is within. When we see ourselves as being God's means to live, then we not only acknowledge the Presence within, but our whole purpose is to reveal that Presence, to let It reveal Itself through all that we think, do, say and feel. We then no longer look for our good from others.

It is when we begin to look for our good from someone else that we are controlled by the belief that the power is outside of our Self. That someone is merely our own consciousness become form. He or she is a reflection of our own Self. If we do not like what we see out there, then we must become more completely in tune with Ideal of God as being the Truth of our Being.

The world is made up of so many traditions. We have to have guidelines and so we go back to yesterday to what has been done before. But those guidelines, those traditions, must be seen as springboards into the new. If we hang on to tradition, we cannot live fully as the unfoldment of our God-Self. The thieves on the cross on either side of Jesus represent the thieves of yesterday and tomorrow. It is always when we are living in yesterday or tomorrow that we have problems.

Many of our holidays are filled with great traditions and so many of us are bound by them that we go through withdrawal pains when we are deprived of them. This dependency upon something outside of our Self reveals that we are of the world. let us choose to live in the NOW. Let us choose to live the Presence of God, and we will be free of these shadows of the mind.

Feeling antagonistic because Easter lilies are not all over the place on Easter Sunday and because we do not sing, "Christ the Lord Is Risen Today," means that we are involved in the world. If we are living the Presence, which is love, then our spirit of adventure permits newness to take place. Those who do not like change are involved in the world. Those who are attached to person, place and thing are involved in the world and are unhappy when those things, and people are not there.

The challenges that come our way are claims upon our potential. Living in the NOW is a great spiritual adventure. It is an adventure of living out of the Self, or being Self-actualized, or realizing that of our own self we can do nothing. In individualizing God we are actively acknowledging that there is a power within that can do anything.

We are only angry when we expect something from others, when we want them to agree with us. We are only frustrated when we look for our good outside of our Self. Our good is all within this Presence, this True and Total Self. Read the newspapers, watch television, look beyond the facts and figures. We must pour into our every moment the expression of our individualization of success, which, then, must manifest the forms of success.

Living in the world is a great opportunity to reveal and express success. Within every purpose there is whoever and whatever is needed to fulfill that purpose. Consciousness must always attract to itself the people and things that are required and representative.

Living and individualizing Self-sufficiency does not mean that others are going to be excluded from our lives. Our living and revealing sufficiency must attract to us all that sufficiency represents. We cannot deny body, we cannot avoid the fruits of our God-expression. Lawyers, doctors, teachers, helpers, workers, friends, lovers, mates, etc. all play a part in the living of the Truth. They are not the power. Truth is the power. We cannot get away from form. Our immortality must always have body. Be in the world, but live each moment in the highest possible way...through revealing the Presence.

When this Presence within us touches our awareness, It touches every single area of our life. Absolutely nothing can exist outside of our consciousness. There is within each one of us this Presence. There is within each one of us this Self that is forever whole and complete, this Self that has never made a mistake, that has never been sick. It is our active at-one-ment with this Self, our acknowledgment of It, that causes It to take over and live through us in terms of Itself. We can call It the Christ, God individualized, our True Self, our God-Self, it doesn't matter. It is still the reality of our Self. Our job is to give it full and total recognition.

When we are not aware of this Self, we are aware of a different concept of self. This concept, which is but a shadow of the mind, is a self that is made up of yesterday's attitudes and yesterday's memories. It is all illusion. When we feel that someone is doing something to us, it is only because we do not like to accept the responsibility for living out of our Self. When we actively are at one with this God-Self, It lives through us and nothing foreign can enter in.

At the ego level we are influenced by everything that we see and hear, failing to realize that what we see and hear represents our own identity. If we are entranced by the gossip of the world, then that is our identity drawing to itself the slander, gossip, opinions and insecurities of the world.

No one can influence God. No one can influence the Christ, this inner individualization of that which we really are. No one can ask anything of It, for It cannot hear the voice of limitation.

If we choose to let this power be an influence in our lives, then we must let go of listening to the world and listen to the voice of this inner Self, this inner teacher of greatness. Our True Self can only understand success, love, abundance and the magnificence that this Self already is.

This Self that lies within us all is always giving signals of Its great purpose. When we surrender to It and let It have Its way, It can and does teach us ideas of our true nature. When we surrender our getting goals then we can begin to hear It speak through our Consciousness with ideas, thoughts and purpose of success.

The world may not necessarily like it when we are experiencing success because our example makes it feel uneasy. But that is the problem of whoever is comparing. We cannot and must not give up our living greatly just so that others will feel comfortable.

Each of us is here to live in a great and magnificent way. This we can do if we dare to individualize success, greatness and magnificence. Mind is our servant. It creates while we direct. Our job is to individually direct Mind in ways of greatness. It is what we individually express and the way that we express it that counts. No one can live for us or direct the law of mind for us. We must accept that responsibility. Using the Science of Mind to demonstrate one thing after another does not teach us to individualize success.

CHAPTER VIII

Spiritual Integrity

Living spiritually or with Spiritual Integrity means that we have surrendered our desire to look to the world for our good. It even means that we have given up our desire and need to get something by means of mental treatment. Our treatments now are simply reminders that we are God's means to live, that we are already complete. Our treatments and meditations are centered on the Kingdom of God within rather than upon all of the things that we need. Anything other than this standard of greatness, is but a shadow of the mind seeking to lead us astray.

Once it is our goal or purpose to live in the highest possible way, which means living the Presence of God, then we cannot go back to living at the human level with all of its indecisions, judgments and uncertainties. Once we choose to live the Presence of God, we can no longer live a completely personal life. When we have awakened to the power of greatness within our Self, It takes over and It has Its own work to do through us. When we let the presence of God be our standard of Self-expression and Self-giving we begin to live out of integrity. Integrity now guides and directs our way.

189

Integrity now reveals to us all that we need to know as we need to know it.

Unless we live out of Integrity, we are going to be involved with people and situations that do not really represent that Integrity. When we go after person place or thing, we have to give up our integrity and do whatever is required to obtain. We may find ourselves doing many things that we do not really want to do, such as lying, cheating, stealing, in order to obtain what we feel we must have. We may find ourselves straying ethically, morally, just so that we can please for the purpose of getting.

The moment that we no longer live out of the Integrity of our Being, we are no longer free to be our own Self. The moment we surrender our right to be our Self, we begin to hate our Self, and thus our every experience is now born out of that Self-hate. Since we always experience everything to the degree that we love or reject our Self, then we must choose to let Integrity be the guiding light in our lives.

When we use our thought to consciously be at one with a certain idea, what really happens? Do we use the idea or does the idea take over and use us? We may select the idea, but the idea is now in charge and it is telling us what to do and how to do it. This happens no matter what the idea is. That is why it is extremely important that Spiritual Integrity be a part of all that we do.

Within every idea that we use is the Power and the Intelligence of the Universe that helps fulfill that idea. Mind can do anything and is all-knowing in how to bring into form any choice that we have made. It creates and draws into our experience anything and everything that is necessary to the idea that is now using us.

When we choose to surrender to the Truth that there is a Power and a Presence always where we are, and we eternally acknowledge It, when we give It our total attention and let It be our reason for living, then that idea will not desert us. It takes over our consciousness and It does whatever needs to be done until we are living that Truth every moment of every day. The integrity of this Presence is absolutely necessary if we are to fulfill our potential, if we are to fulfill our reason for being.

Just because you are now reading this book means that there is something within you that desires to live the Presence, that desires to live your life in the highest possible way. Having read up to this point you cannot ever be free of the idea that there is a great power within, that you and I are God's means to live. When we are searching for a way to live life more completely, Mind provides an answer. The answer is the Real Self, the True Self, that Self that can do anything and do it greatly. That Self is taking over within us right now and we must open ourselves up to the way.

The more completely that we surrender to this Self, this power, through our active acknowledgment of It, the more quickly does It become an authority and power in our life. When we have caught a glimpse of the greatness within our Self, never again can we fully live at the begging level of trying to add to our Self by looking for our good outside of our Self. Never again can we be free of that inner voice that says, "The Presence of God is right where I am. It IS my Self. I am living out of Spiritual Integrity now and always."

In living out of Spiritual Integrity there is something within us that is never again going to let us procrastinate or rest in the status quo. This something within us will make us uneasy every time that we try to get rather than to give. Spiritual Integrity tells us that we are here not to live materially, but spiritually. This does not mean that we will not have things in our life, because the law of our Being is always in action and we always have the things that reflect our level of Awareness. Living out of Spiritual Integrity means that we will have quality things and quality people and that we live in a less complicated way.

Living out of Spiritual Integrity means that we now recognize that we are already complete and that it is our purpose to let this completeness shine through all that we do. Now we realize that all that we have been trying to get is nothing but a shadow of the mind and this need does not really exist because we are already complete.

In living our Spiritual Integrity we must accept totally that we are already whole, total, perfect, complete. Regardless of the idea that we choose, that idea that we live we must experience. We are here now to select ideas of greatness rather than smallness. Spiritual Integrity is choosing those ideas that reflect the nature of our God-Self and simply by-passing those that do not. We are here on this plane of expression for too short a period of time—no matter how long that may be—to waste our time and energies with goals and ideas of mediocrity. We must dare to go all the way and soar with the power of our Total Self.

In living our lives out of Integrity, we realize that we do not need anything from anyone. Yes, it is true that we must receive love in order to be fulfilled, but Integrity means that we are love in action always and thus the receiving is automatic. Needing things and people turns us into beggars and what we beg we will never really have. Yes, we may get some hand-outs, but they do not satisfy for very long. In living out of Integrity we know that the law of our Being is taking care of the details and that we can let go of our every human concern.

Now our purpose is to live with Integrity, and now is the time to do it. The law of cause and effect is always in action and so the things will always be there corresponding to what it is that we are expressing. With Spiritual Integrity we are dedicating ourselves to giving the highest of our Self to all that we do. We go the extra mile and receive accordingly.

Integrity always has its own purpose. That purpose is always great. Spiritual Integrity is, of course, based upon the greatness and completeness of the Self. It is God being individualized. Its purpose is to share, to reveal, to live the Presence of God. When this is our goal, our purpose, Spiritual Integrity becomes the fibre of our Being, the truth of our character, and the power behind our motivation to give, not to get. We always have what we give and since what we are trying to get is always kept from us, then it is practical to direct the law of mind with Integrity.

We are always trying to get when we concern ourselves with what others think of us or seem to be saying about us. When we choose to have Spiritual Integrity, then It takes over and takes complete charge of our Self-expression. Integrity is now using us. It uses us and provides whatever is required to live life greatly. We are the ones, however, who must make the choice. We cannot live a choiceless life and we must not permit others to make our choices for us.

We so often do not use Mind in ways that can serve us greatly. Or, let us say, we direct Mind in ways that do not serve the ideas of Greatness completely. Mind is our servant. Mind will give to us whatever it is that we claim. It cannot say no. However, when we go after things, even in prayer or treatment, we are the servant of those things because we are directing Mind at the level of begging. The things are now controlling us even though it is Mind that produces them. The things that we must have now cause us to do things that have nothing to do with Integrity.

In trying to get we are directing Mind in ways that

can only limit us. In living out of a desperate sense of need we are giving up our Spiritual Integrity because we now have to do whatever someone demands of us, now we have to do whatever things demand of us.

Since this is the way it is, then let us choose to direct Mind by means of our Spiritual Integrity, letting each day be to us what we are to our God-Self. Today is meant to be lived joyously and enthusiastically, but it is always up to us. It is to us whatever we choose.

Since God is perfection, abundance, love, order, harmony, energy, beauty, success, peace, and is eternally complete, then our Spiritual Integrity demands that this is what we express. Mind is our servant, It helps us to live with Integrity when we choose to live that Integrity. When we acknowledge this ideal and act as though it is so, then we are proving that we mean business, and Mind creates accordingly for us.

So many people say that their intentions are always of the highest, but as they get involved with their day they forget to remember Who and What they really are. They say that they are inspired when they hear lectures and read books, but as soon as they get out into the world the inspiration fades away. It may last for a day, or even a week, but that is about it. However, Mind is here to help us always. We can direct Mind to remind us of Who and What we are AT ALL TIMES. It is simply a matter of giving it direction. To say that this cannot be done is a shadow of the mind.

We are not here to beg or hope. We are here to KNOW. Our positive statements of Truth are used as reminders, but unless we use them, we go on as before. Since we choose our every experience in one way or another, we must accept the responsibility to make positive choices. Many people say that they are too depressed to make positive choices, but even then they are making a choice—to stay depressed. Depression is always a choice, as is everything that we experience. When we live out of Spiritual Integrity we cannot possibly make the choice to be depressed.

Every challenge, every so-called problem, is really an opportunity to be Self-aware. The problem says to us that we have strayed, that we are "off Principle." That's all it is. We need not be ashamed of making a mistake. But should we choose to stay in the problem, as so many people do, then the only thing that will get us out of it is to deliberately make another choice. Thinking of it as a problem is also a shadow of the mind, for, in reality, it is but a lesson to learn, an opportunity to be more completely Self-aware.

Spiritual Integrity accepts the growth choice—the opportunity to give or to reveal the nature of God in a larger way. When the challenge comes along, Mind is still our servant. The opportunity to remind ourselves of our True purpose has been created along with the golden chance for us to live the Presence more completely. It is truly great what Mind can do for us, in what It can give through us and to us.

God does not give the gifts of people, money or things. It gives of Itself through ideas that then manifest as person, situation or thing. Our demonstration is not the money, but the greater idea, the consciousness of abundance. Our demonstration is not the house, but the Truth, the Spiritual Integrity that evolves as the house, or whatever else represents that which we are living and revealing.

It is only through Spiritual Integrity that we attain and maintain the things in our life with ease and love, blessing not only our own self, but all in our lives.

When we are treating for things, we do not live spiritually. We are, instead, living materialistically and

195

we must suffer the consequences of that approach, for it brings frustration, anxiety, fear and even anger.

Although we demonstrate the thing or the person we want, having gone after it, we are not free to be our Self, to live our own life. In going after someone we have to do whatever is necessary to keep that person in our life. It may not be worth it. That someone we go after is controlling us. He or she is dominating our thought and our actions. We have demonstrated them at the level of getting rather than of Being.

What good is being in a relationship where you are not free to be the uniqueness that you are? What good is being in any situation where you always have to agree? What good is giving up all of your special interests and your integrity just so you might pacify and please the other person. If we already were the consciousness that deserves the ideal mate, we would already have him or her in our life in a creative way.

The freedom to be our own Self, to think for our Self, to live out of our Self, is absolutely necessary in creative relationships. We are not here to be copycats and to let others do our thinking for us. The freedom to be wherever we need to be in order to fulfill our work, our purpose, is necessary at all times, and this cannot happen if we are a slave to the people in our life, to our house, to our possessions. When we live out of Spiritual Integrity we may rock the boat, but that is what boats are for, Spiritual Integrity demands that we be different.

What good is having anything or anyone if we are not free to be our unique and special Self? What good is having money if we are afraid to spend it? What good is having that physically attractive person in our life if they are continually throwing temper tantrums in order to get their own way? If this is the way it is going, can that person be our true demonstration when that is not our true purpose or true goal?

In going after the particular person and winning him or her at all costs, we no longer are free. In going after the money we are no longer free. In going after the job and having to have it no matter what, we are no longer free. In going after anything we are being controlled and our strings are being pulled by others. Spiritual Integrity does not permit us to live at the level of effect, we live at the level of pure cause.

Our real purpose is to live fully and completely at all times. Our true purpose is to live out of a sense of completeness and to be our own unique Self in action. Our purpose is to be true to the integrity of our Being. Nothing is worth giving up our personhood. When we are always true to our Spiritual Integrity Mind must automatically bring into our life those who correspond, those who help us live that Integrity.

Our whole reason for being is to permit this Power, this Presence of God, to do Its work—whatever that is— by means of all that we think, say and do. When we actively acknowledge this Presence, It may send us across the world into new and different places, into new and greater responsibilities, into new and different expressions of our Self.

God is always moving forward, not backwards. It never stands still. When we are guided to move forward, we must move. What good is knowing that there is an inner Intelligence if we are going to ignore the guidance that we receive from within? Many people treat or pray for a Divine Purpose, a reason for being that is for the highest good of all. When they make their demonstration and have an opportunity to move forward, to use their talents in greater ways, they turn it down because it means that they would have to uproot and go somewhere else. It means that they would have to leave their friends, sell their house, etc.

When we receive our inner messages and fail to use them we cut ourselves off from the Source. When we do not listen to our Inner Self, we are going backwards and it will probably manifest as some kind of bodily pain, financial lack, diminishing of self-esteem because we are now directing Mind in terms of less rather than more.

We have no right to say no to the forward flow of life. We have no right to stop our unfoldment. We may say, "Well of course I have the right to say no. I can do whatever I want. I think for myself." Yes, that is true, but when we choose to live the Presence, to live Spiritual Integrity, when we must surrender to It and let It take over. Thinking for our Self is really listening to our inner voice.

If the inner voice of Truth, of our Spiritual Integrity guides and directs our way, then we MOVE. We go wherever we are guided to go. When we serve an idea of greatness, that idea points the way. If we say no, then we are saying yes to a different idea and we must reap the consequences of whatever idea we choose. In letting Spiritual Integrity take charge of our life, we must fulfill the work that It needs to do though us.

As we are living out of Spiritual Integrity our daily life becomes an entirely different experience. We find ourselves being true to our Self rather than being at the beck and call of the world. We find ourselves no longer reacting to what is going on "out there" because now the excitement and the power is "within."

When we are always giving thanks for the things and the people in our life, for our health and our wealth and everything that has been given to us, we are, in essence, saying that our good is in things, in people. Everything that has ever come to us we deserve by right of consciousness. All of the people in our lives we deserve because the law of our Being has brought them to us. We are experiencing all through our state of mind. Instead of being grateful for the results, we should be grateful for the cause. We must be grateful for knowing Who and What we really are. We should give thanks for knowing that the law of our Self is always in action and that our Self is already complete.

Be grateful for Spiritual Integrity that is guiding and directing our way. The law of attraction automatically takes care of the details, and even though something seems to be coming through someone else, from someone else, we must be aware that it is really coming from our own consciousness. The power of our Self is always at work and when that Self has Spiritual Integrity, then that is what we are going to experience.

At the level of Spiritual Integrity, our way is dedicated to living love, which is the Presence. In this approach we are dedicated to doing Its work, to revealing Its Integrity in all that we do and the way that we do it.

Many people say, "I hate my job. I hate where I am. I hate my boss. I am disgusted with this job and it is not good enough for me." Of course, what we hate we always maintain. If we hate our jobs, we must ask ourselves why we are there. We must realize that we only hate it because we are not giving the best of ourselves to it. Wherever we are always reflects our own consciousness, our level of Integrity. This kind of emotion always ties us to the object of our feeling. Even if we run away, we take ourselves with us, the hate, the feelings of inadequacy, and we pour all of this into whatever we are doing. Running away always means that we will experience what we are running away from all over again.

We must always begin where we are, no matter where that is. Another mate, another job, another house, are not the answer. Our Spiritual Integrity is. We take ourselves with us wherever we go. Consciousness always becomes form no matter where we are. We must always begin with our Self WHERE WE PRESENTLY ARE. Spiritual Integrity must be attained and lived right where we are at the present moment. We cannot afford to hate anything or anyone for that hate is a way of directing Mind that has dire consequences for our own Self.

The person that we hate represents something within our own Self. It represents a shadow of the mind but always manifests as a person. If we do not know the Truth for those we hate, the door is kept closed to our own good. That person we dislike represents something within our own Self that needs to be healed. As we pray for our enemies this expression of love quickly brings into our life the good that has evaded us. If we have not been demonstrating our good, if some area of our life seems to be incomplete, it is because we have someone in our life whom we dislike, hate, envy or criticize.

We must awaken to Who and What we truly are right where we are so that we can love all. Only by giving the highest of our Self to ALL that we are doing—where we are in the present moment—are we going to be free to move forward into the next step of our unfoldment.

When I was selecting a new home several years ago I made the rounds with my real estate agent of those homes that were available and on the market. It was amazing to see the great number of houses that were not in Divine Order. It was not difficult to understand why those houses were not moving and had been on the market for some time. To me it was inconceivable that anyone would put their house up for sale unless the house was clean, painted, and in order. In some cases it appeared as though the owners had lived in the house until it got to be such a mess that they themselves could no longer stand it and so their solution was to move.

But who wants to inherit that kind of a situation?

It is the law of life that in order to demonstrate a better, larger, more beautiful and luxurious home, we have to build the consciousness of it first of all. This means that we must begin where we are. We must make the most of where we are. We must build consciousness by establishing order, love, beauty, harmony and order where we are. In trying to camouflage and hide the mess we are in, hoping that others will not notice, we are directing Mind to give to us this same type of experience wherever we go. We always take ourselves with us and a consciousness of disorder always goes along and recreates itself regardless of where we are.

There are those who let their checking accounts get into such a mess that they can no longer handle them, and their solution is to close out that account and open a new one in a different bank. But the process starts all over again immediately and so they go from one bank to another.

If we are to move into the greater, we have to be the greater in action right were we are. We are always directing Mind by what we are NOW doing and NOW revealing. The house that we are now in must be in perfect order before we can really release it, before the law of love and harmony move us into our greater experience. If we are living our Spiritual Integrity we will enjoy life more than ever and that Integrity can only go before us and prepare the way.

Spiritual Integrity keeps us busy, but it does not exhaust us. Spiritual Integrity begins in what we are now doing, in the way that we are now living, in what we are expressing right where we are. This is the way that we are directing the law of Mind.

When we are dissatisfied with our present jobs and do not like the situation, we think that the solution is to quit and then go and look for something else. There is nothing wrong in moving forward and upward, but wherever we go is just an extension of where we are. Taking drugs, getting drunk or using tranquilizers never solves anything. They are an escape and when we "come to" our situation is still the same. In running away from where we are we are still going to experience our consciousness. Only as we are expressing our Spiritual Integrity, our God-Self, is it going to be really creative to move forward to the next golden opportunity. If we are pouring out love, joy, self-assertiveness, enthusiasm, health, wealth and success into whatever we are NOW doing, then all of this action must cause Mind to create the next forward step, the larger opportunity.

Putting our house in order means that we are filling our consciousness with the qualities of God, and, above all, God-expression. Until we have done this we cannot move forward, even if we physically quit one job and take another. As our present home reveals Divine Order, then we are ready to move into the new home which reflects our growing and expanding consciousness of order, beauty and love. We always have to begin right where we are.

Running away is NEVER the answer. If we receive offers of other jobs, even a much better one, we must make sure that we are not accepting just to get away from where we are. Being excited about what we are now doing is the only way to demonstrate a greater opportunity that truly reflects where we are. It may be that we are very happy where we are and would never dream of going anywhere else. Even so, we are still always meant to move forward. It is the law of life that we do not stay in the same experience for too long a period of time. We cannot stay too long at the fair. Accepting a larger opportunity to serve is a lot different from running from one job to another because we are trying to get away from the unhappiness we are now in.

Spiritual Integrity can be ours if we let our guidelines be taken from our Ideal Self, our God-Self. It means that we give the very highest of our Self to all that we are doing. It does not begin tomorrow because tomorrow never arrives. We are always living today. Somewhere else can only be an extension of where we now are.

Today is the time to begin living the Presence of God, of living and revealing our Spiritual Integrity. When we acknowledge Who and What we truly are and then begin acting as though it is so, we are on the way. We must take positive statements, affirmations, claim them and then move them into action. We are only as good as the idea that we are expressing right now.

The personal or human way is to try to get something for nothing. But that never really works because it is the law of life that we always have to earn our own good by right of consciousness. This means that we must do our own work, our own thinking, our own living. We never get anything for nothing.

It may seem as though there are those in our life or in the public eye who are not using Integrity and that they are getting ahead. Remember, however, that those people are also directing Mind in terms of whatever they are doing and the way that they are doing it, and if there is no Integrity there, the law of Mind will find ways for them to suffer the consequences. It is not up to us to reprimand them or to try to punish them. The law of their Being will take care of them, while our judgment will take care of us.

People are what they are. What they are doing reveals where they are at in consciousness. It is the only way that they can behave right now. To try to force them to behave in ways that is against their patterns of Being can only end up in frustration. At the present moment they cannot comprehend any other way. They must eventually awaken to the law of their being. It will happen. We cannot make it happen for them. Spiritual Integrity demands that we mind our own business. Spiritual Integrity, for us, is not what others are doing. It is what we ourselves are living right now.

There will always be people behaving in ways that do not represent our own Integrity. Those who are in our life are here for some reason. But not for us to whip them into shape. If we are busy living out of love, then we will have the people of love in our lives and our own expression of love will heal and bless. How others choose to live their lives is simply none of our business.

Our own experience is created out of our Self, not someone else's Self. Our experience is created out of what we are now doing, not out of what someone else is doing. We must release the people in our lives so that they can be with us in a loving way. When we release we do not kick them out of our life. We simply release them as being cause to our experience and we get busy with our own doing and living. Spiritual Integrity has to do with the building of our own consciousness, not someone elses.

Spiritual Integrity takes us away from praying or treating for things or for health, wealth and success. Spiritual Integrity is the active recognition that we are already complete. In this recognition Mind attracts and creates all that corresponds. This is forever going on. Treating to get something is a great denial of the power that we already are.

In our Spiritual Integrity we also recognize the sufficiency of others and we do whatever is necessary to help their sufficiency be expressed. We do not give advice because we know that they have their own answers. We do not demand that they accept our viewpoint and agree with us because we know that they are unique and have a right to their own beliefs. Spiritual Integrity recognizes that each person is an individualization of God and that each has his or her own answer, his or her own purpose and reason for being.

Every time that we give advice to someone we are in effect saying that they have no intelligence. We are telling them that we know better than they. But how could we know better when they are different, when they are they and we are we? Their uniqueness is not a replica of ours. Even a small child has his own answer and we are not helping him to awaken to his sufficiency by continually telling him what to think and never listening to what he is trying to tell us.

Spiritual Integrity says that God is everywhere present—EVEN WITHIN THE PEOPLE WE DO NOT LIKE.

Either we believe in God or we don't. If we do, then we must release the people in our world to their own inner voice, to their own lessons to learn, to their own challenges. When we impose anything upon others we are saying that we do not believe in God. Spiritual Integrity causes me to recognize the great power within you and to give you back your challenge. I help by knowing that there is that within you that knows what to do.

Our Spiritual Integrity does not permit us to go out into the world and behave in ways that deny perfection, order, abundance or the eternality of life. Our Spiritual Integrity does not force others to give to us what we want. We know that our good is to be found only within our own Self.

Many people pride themselves in knowing all of the tricks of the trade as to how to get what they want, as to how to get others to give in, as to how to win by intimidation, etc. But that is revealing that they believe their good is outside of their Self. That is saying that they do not believe in God, in themselves.

Since Mind will not permit anything to enter into our experience except that which represents our Self, then we do not have to resort to intimidation or power struggles if we are using Spiritual Integrity. When we are the Integrity of our Self in action we do not have to defend ourselves or try to convince others that they are wrong and that we are right.

In acknowledging that God is the only power, then we know that each person in our lives is right for him or her and it is not our business how they should live or what the answers are that they receive from within their Self. We may feel that it very definitely is our business if someone we love wants to do something that we ourselves do not want to do. We cannot, however, believe that we own people or that they should sacrifice their needs so that our own can be fulfilled, or vice versa.

There is always an answer, and when several of us are involved there is an answer that is right for the highest good of all. This means for the Integrity of all. We cannot have a WE experience if we give up our lives for others or demand that they give up theirs for us. It takes two whole people to make a WE. We must be true to our own Self, to our own Integrity and we must help the people in our lives do likewise. When we are all living out of our Spiritual Integrity the law of our Being will make whatever adjustments are necessary at the visible level.

Spiritual Integrity will not permit us to live in the guilts of yesterday. We have all made mistakes. So what? But those mistakes of yesterday belong to yesterday. Spiritual Integrity causes us to live in the NOW. If God is all there is and God never sits in judgment upon Itself, then our living the Presence of God frees us forever of any guilt about yesterday because today is all there is. God is today. Spiritual Integrity will not let us go back to the shadows of the mind, the shadows of yesterday.

Spiritual Integrity keeps us centered on the giving of our God-Self to the present moment, regardless of who is in that moment.

There is something within each of us that has work to do, that has a divine purpose. It has something to give, to live and express, and by God, BY GOD, it is now unfolding, it is now moving into expression when we are free of the shadows of the mind and are living Spiritual Integrity. The greatness, totality, magnificence, the genius that God is as each of us is now alive within us and never again can we be free of that recognition, of that power.

Spritual Integrity is already within us. All we have to do is to give It our recognition, our attention. As we do this our motivation is instantly one of serving rather than getting. There is that within us that can give quality to life and thus cause Mind to create a world of beauty and love. Quality is a lot better than quantity. Let us permit Mind to attract to us only that which represents beauty, abundance, and our Integrity. Let Spiritual Integrity come forth, by to the best of our ability living the Presence of God in all that we think, say and do.

THIS IS THE BEGINNING.